Cover: *St Cecilia, by John Melhuish Strudwick (1849-1937)*

*Boniface by Alfred Rethel (1816-59)*

# A Book of Saints

James Cochrane

# Contents

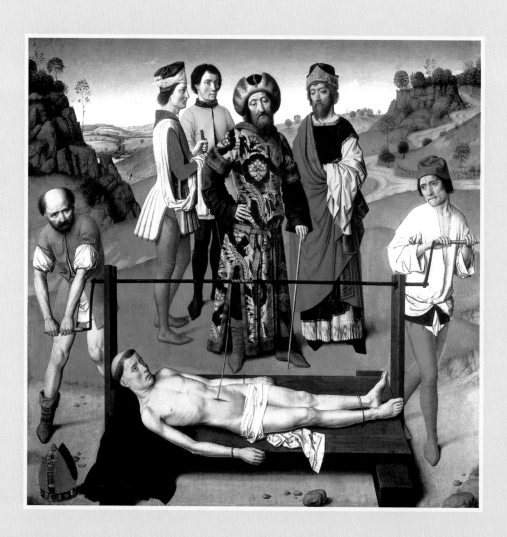

*Martyrdom of St Erasmus by Dieric Bouts (1410/20-75)*

# Foreword

What are saints? In the Christian tradition the word has been used in a variety of senses over the centuries. When St Paul, for example, addresses himself to the saints at Ephesus or Philippi he is clearly referring to the living communities of faithful Christians in those places. The word was used in the same way by some of the Protestant sects of the sixteenth century and later. Nowadays, when the word is used collectively it can refer to all those Christians who have died and are now in Heaven – the 'saints who from their labours rest'. Saints in that sense presumably include at least some of our own deceased loved ones, and Christians may hope to be one day among their number, but the identities of most are, for the time being, known only to God. However, since the earliest days of Christendom the churches have declared that certain named individuals have lived or died in such a way that they are assuredly in Heaven; these are the saints as exemplified by the men and women in this book.

For the first thousand years or so of Christianity, sanctification was often a matter, more or less, of popular local acclamation. Only after the tenth century did it gradually become centralized under the control of the pope and the patriarchate of the Orthodox churches. Since the seventeenth century the Roman Catholic church has followed a process of formal canonization involving a prolonged and minute inquiry into the candidate's life.

It is important to recognize that the process of canonization – which simply means inclusion in a canon, or officially approved list – does not *make* someone a saint; it is a formal recognition that that person *was* a saint in his or her lifetime. Being declared a saint does not mean that the person has lived a flawless life, even if that were possible. It is rather that he or she has acted at a heroic level of Christian devotion to an extent that could only be attained by the grace of Christ. It is this, rather than evidence for or against moral perfection, that the long process of inquiry seeks to establish. Journalists have sought to find flaws in the character of Mother Teresa, but if and when she is canonized it will not be because she has achieved perfection but because of a lifetime of devotion to the Christ she saw in the poor and wretched of Calcutta. Conversely, Maximilian Kolbe was canonized in 1982, not for his lifetime's achievement, but for his heroic self-sacrifice at Auschwitz in August 1941. Similarly, at the time of writing the Russian Orthodox church has announced the canonization of Tsar Nicholas II and his wife and children, not because they led blameless lives, but because of the way they met their savage and brutal deaths.

The idea of evidence of the grace of Christ in a saint's life is one of the principles that link the Christian idea of sainthood with that of the other great religions of the world. The definition common to them all is that a saint has a special relationship with god, or with the gods, or with the realm of the sacred in general. The evidence for that relationship is to be seen in miracles, whether they are performed by the saint or are miraculous signs associated with him or her. The miracles are often what we would describe as supernatural – for example healings of the apparently incurable, or levitation, or the appearance of the stigmata of Christ's wounds on the saint's body, or remarkable natural phenomena such as strange events in the heavens. They may also be, and in the modern Christian church tend to be, examples of miraculous courage or miraculous devotion and self-sacrifice, acts beyond the capacities of unaided human beings.

How many recognized Christian saints are there? The answer is that there is no definitive canon. The latest edition of *Butler's Lives of the Saints* contains over 2,500 names; the *Roman Martyrology* has some 4,500 and does not claim to be exhaustive; the *Biblioteca Sanctorum*, published by the Lateran University in Rome, has almost 1000 for January alone. The martyrologies of Ireland and Wales name thousands of saints, including some three hundred all called Colman; in many cases, a name, a place and a feast-day is all that is recorded of these Celtic saints. Additionally there are the calendars and martyrologies of the Orthodox churches of, for example, Greece and Russia. The total number must be very large indeed.

Of these thousands of saints, this book contains brief lives of about one hundred of the better known or more interesting, arranged, unusually, in chronological rather than calendar or alphabetical order. The reader will soon see that the great majority of them fall into the first seventeen centuries and that their numbers drop off sharply thereafter. The reason for this is quite simple: the majority of the most famous saints, those who seemed to demand inclusion, lived and died in those earlier centuries. Furthermore, although the process of canonization continues – the present pope has been very active in this regard – it has been much slower and more cautious in considering the cases of candidates from the eighteenth century to the present day. And of course, since the Reformation, the Protestant churches, while continuing to revere at least some of the saints, have not chosen to add to their number. As a result of these factors there are fewer recognized saints from relatively modern times.

Arranged chronologically, these representative lives of the saints may be seen as a kind of history of Christendom, from St John the Baptist and St Joseph to the twentieth century. Read in this way, what impression do they give, what might they teach us of the essentials of Christianity through twenty centuries of historical change? To an open-minded reader of the twenty-first century, some of the lives of the early saints in particular might suggest notions of bigotry or fanaticism, and there are certainly plentiful examples of saints who condemned others to the scaffold and the stake. On the other hand, the eagerness with which the early martyrs themselves sought torture and death can strike us as deeply morbid; it must surely have been based on an absolute certainty of instant admission to Heaven, recalling the example of Islamic fundamentalist suicide bombers in our own time. Christian scholars in modern times have questioned the veracity of those accounts of ingenious and horrifying tortures at the hands of pagan oppressors, not least because exactly the same stories are regularly attached to two or more different martyred saints. To some extent they have to be seen as propaganda for the view that the pre-Christian Roman world was wholly without love or decency, a view that few questioned before the Renaissance; they might be seen too as a kind of permitted sex-and-violence pornography, epitomized in thousands of engravings that graphically depict the mutilation of young women, or, for example, in the obvious eroticism of paintings of the martyrdom of St Sebastian.

The stories of saints who withdraw from the world and their fellow men and renounce all material comforts and possessions in order to achieve personal salvation and spiritual wisdom may strike the modern reader as examples of a particularly selfish kind of individualism. But saints of this kind appear in all the world's great religions, and during their lives they were not regarded as selfish but, on the contrary, were revered by large numbers of ordinary people, who must have felt that they benefited from their existence. Perhaps that benefit had something to do with the comforting assurance they gave that the realm of the sacred was not remote and uncaring but could dwell among men, and in men. For this reason, after these saints died, their remains, and the things and places associated with them, continued to be revered for centuries afterwards. And it has to be remembered that the hermitic tradition in Christendom developed into monasticism, with its incalculable benefits, not just in preserving intellectual and artistic culture and in civilizing Christendom's secular rulers but also in a wide range of practical matters, from medicine and architecture to vinification, brewing and husbandry.

From the earliest times in the history of Christianity it is possible to find the kind of saint who is more immediately attractive to the modern sensibility - a person perhaps best described by Bernard of Clairvaux in the 12th century in these words: 'seen to be good and charitable, living as a man among men, holding back nothing for himself but using his every gift for the common good; he looks on himself as every man's debtor, alike to friend and foe, to the wise and the foolish. Such a one, being wholly humble, benefits all, is dear to God and man'. The very first martyr, Stephen, was engaged in charitable work among the Christian community at Jerusalem. St Paul, who as a young man held the coats of the men who stoned Stephen to death, later wrote: 'If I...have not charity, I am nothing'.

This is by no means the only definition of sainthood, but it is perhaps the kind we most easily recognize and respond to, and many examples of this kind of saintliness will be found within the pages of this book. When we read of the men and women who, as priests and nuns and monks, but also as laymen, devoted themselves to the material and spiritual needs of the sick and the poor, we should remember two things: first of all, that the sick and the poor included many whom their fellow men regarded as both repellent and frightening; and secondly that it is in only the last hundred years or so, and only in the advanced industrial world, that other institutions, most notably the state, have given any attention to even the physical needs of the poorest and weakest members of society.

All Christians believe in the notion of salvation through Christ. Some, but perhaps not all, go on to ask: 'But what shall I do when I am saved?' The answer is: 'Love thy neighbour'. To the next question - 'But who is my neighbour?' - the answer is 'All of humanity' or even, perhaps, 'All of God's creation'. The saints we most admire are probably those those who have lived by those answers, personally risking disease and death. The principle of saintliness they represent joins the essence of Christianity with what is best in all the religions of the world.

*John the Baptist by Alexander Andrejevich Ivanov (1806-58)*

# John the Baptist (24 June)

The forerunner of Jesus Christ was the son of Zachary, a priest of the Temple in Jerusalem, and Elizabeth, a cousin of Mary, the mother of Jesus. Both were elderly and childless when an angel announced to Zachary that Elizabeth would bear him a child. John appears in the New Testament as an adult, dressed in animal skins and living on locusts and wild honey, calling on sinners to repent and baptizing them in the river Jordan. Many followed him, but he preached, 'I baptize you with water, but He who is coming after me is mightier than I, whose sandals I am not fit to carry. He will baptize you with the Holy Spirit and with fire'. When Jesus Himself asked John to baptize Him, he did so reluctantly. John said of Him, 'Behold the Lamb of God, who takes away the sins of the world'.

Soon after this, John entered into political controversy when he denounced Herod Antipas, the tetrarch of Galilee, for unlawfully taking Herodias, his half-brother's wife, in marriage. For this he was thrown into prison. It seems that Herod had no intention of proceeding further against him, but at a banquet, when Herodias's daughter danced before him and his courtiers, he rashly promised to give her anything she wished. Guided by Herodias, Salome asked for the head of John the Baptist. Obliged to keep a vow he had made before witnesses, Herod consented to the beheading of John, and his head was presented to Salome on a platter. His body was then taken away by his followers and placed in a tomb.

# Joseph (19 March)

Nothing is known about the husband of Mary and foster-father of Jesus save what we are told in the Gospels. He was of the house of David, that is, of royal descent, but a poor man, who worked as a carpenter, perhaps as a builder, in the town of Nazareth. Although later legends and countless religious paintings depict him as elderly, he was in all probability a young man when he became betrothed to Mary. Discovering that she was pregnant, he seems to have been more concerned for her than for himself, but an angel came to him in a vision and told him not to fear to take her as his wife, for 'That which is conceived in her is of the Holy Spirit. She will bear a son and you will call Him Jesus'.

Joseph is described as an 'upright man'. Certainly he seems to have been a loving husband and foster-father. Learning from another angelic vision that Herod planned to kill the infant Jesus, he took his family into Egypt and thus saved His life. He again showed his concern when the boy Jesus was thought to be lost after a visit to Jerusalem for Passover when He was twelve years old. We are told nothing of Joseph's later life, and his death is not recorded, but he was certainly not present at the crucifixion.

# Andrew (30 November)

The first apostle to be called by Jesus was a fisherman of Galilee. He brought with him his brother Simon, who became Peter. Andrew is mentioned several times in the Gospels as one of the leading disciples, along with Peter, James and John. Nothing is known for certain about his life after the resurrection and ascension, but there is a tradition that he preached in Scythia and Greece and may have gone to Constantinople, and that he was crucified on an x-shaped cross in the year 60.

Andrew is the patron saint of Scotland, whose national flag bears his saltire cross, and of Russia.

*Detail from The Apostle Andrew by Georges de la Tour (1593-1652)*

# James the Greater

(25 July)

J ames the Greater, the brother of John, is so called to distinguish him from the younger disciple of the same name. He was a Galilean and a fisherman, summoned with his brother to follow Jesus when they were fishing with their father one day on Lake Genesareth. Jesus called the two brothers Boanerges, 'Sons of Thunder', supposedly from their impetuous natures and hot tempers. From time to time He had to rebuke them, but they were, with Peter, the apostles who were closest to Him at the beginning of His Passion.

There is a strong tradition in Spain that James went there to preach after the Ascension, and that after his martyrdom in Jerusalem in 44 his remains were taken to Compostela, which in the middle ages became the greatest of all Christian shrines and remains a centre of pilgrimage to this day.

*St James the Greater by Benvenuto Tisi da Garofalo (1481-1559)*

# Mary Magdalen (22 July)

Mary of Magdala is the woman who became Jesus' follower after He healed her of 'seven devils' and who may have given Him and his disciples financial support. She was one of the women present at the crucifixion, and according to Mark's Gospel it was to her that the risen Christ first appeared after she went to His tomb and found it empty.

In the Western Christian tradition she is commonly identified with the unnamed woman who 'was a sinner' and who anointed Jesus' feet and with Mary of Bethany, the sister of Martha. This identification has long been questioned by scholars and is not accepted by the Eastern Church, but in the West the belief that Mary was a reformed prostitute has resulted in her being seen as the outstanding exemplar of penitence.

# Matthew (21 September)

The Matthew traditionally regarded as the author of the first Gospel was a tax farmer for the Roman administration and therefore probably a man of considerable wealth, working at Capernaum when he was called by Jesus. He may also have been called Levi. His Gospel alone tells the story of the Magi who followed a star to the cradle of the infant Jesus and is the only one to use the word 'church'. It is believed that Matthew proclaimed Christianity to his fellow Jews and there is a tradition that he was martyred somewhere in Ethiopia.

*St Matthew, Lindisfarne Gospels (698-700)*

*St Mary Magdalen with St Dominic and St Bernard, by Nicolas Borras (1530-1610)*

# Philip and James (3 May)

*The Apostle Philip by Georges de la Tour (1593-1652)*

Two apostles, Philip and James the Less (or Younger) share this feast-day. Philip came from Bethsaida and was called by Jesus the day after Peter and Andrew. From his several appearances in the Gospel of St John (his name is merely mentioned in the other three Gospels) he emerges as an amiable, practical, somewhat literal-minded figure. Jesus is described as testing him, perhaps teasing, when, before the feeding of the five thousand, He asks him 'Whence shall we buy bread that these may eat?' and Philip replies 'Two hundred pennyworth of bread is not sufficient for them that every one may take a little'. And on the evening before the Passion, it is Philip who says to Jesus, 'Lord, show us the Father, and it is enough for us', eliciting the reply: 'Philip, he that seeth me seeth the Father also'. Nothing is known for certain of his life thereafter, but there is a tradition that he preached in Phrygia and died at Hierapolis.

James the Less is so called to distinguish him from the senior disciple, James the Greater. He is described in the New Testament as the 'son of Alphaeus' and as 'the brother of the Lord'; the latter appellation may mean that he was Jesus' cousin, but almost certainly not that he was literally his brother. It is commonly believed that he was the James who led the Christian community at Jerusalem after Jesus' ascension and who was martyred there by stoning to death.

# Peter (29 June)

Peter, 'the prince of the Apostles', was a Galilean, a fisherman, and the brother of Andrew, with whom he was called by Jesus to be a 'fisher of men'. He was originally called Simon, but Jesus gave him as a name the word which in Aramaic means 'rock', and whose Greek equivalent gives us the English name 'Peter'. His supremacy among the apostles was confirmed when Jesus said to him 'Thou art Peter and upon this rock I will build my church' and conferred on him 'the keys of the kingdom of Heaven'. When Jesus was arrested Peter denied knowledge of Him three times to the servants of the high-priest, but after the resurrection and the ascension he redeemed himself by taking on the leadership of the Christian community with commitment and courage, performing miracles, admitting Gentiles and making missionary journeys to Samaria, Antioch and elsewhere. By tradition he went to Rome and was martyred there during the reign of the emperor Nero by crucifixion, head downwards at his own request, and his body was buried under what is now the altar of the Vatican basilica.

*St Peter by William Holman Hunt (1827-1910)*

# Thomas

Thomas is also known by the Greek name 'Didymus', both names meaning 'the Twin', but he is best known to Christians as 'Doubting Thomas', from the incident described in John's Gospel. Thomas was not present with the other disciples when Jesus appeared to them after His resurrection. When they reported what had happened, he said, 'Except I shall see in His hands the print of the nails, and put my finger in the place of the nails, and put my hand into His side, I will not believe'. Eight days later he was present when the risen Christ appeared among them and spoke directly to him, saying, 'Put in thy finger hither, and see my hands; and bring hither thy hand and put it into my side. And be not faithless, but believing'. Then Thomas fell at His feet, crying, 'My Lord and my God!' It was to Thomas also that, at the Last Supper, Jesus spoke the words, 'I am the way, the truth and the life'.

Nothing is known for certain about Thomas's subsequent life, but there is an ancient tradition that he went to India, made many converts and founded churches there. To this day there are Christians in southern India who call themselves 'St Thomas's Christians' and whose liturgy involves the use of Syriac, a language he may well have spoken.

*The Incredulity of St Thomas by Giovanni Francesco Toscani (1370-1430)*

# Mark (25 April)

The author of St Mark's Gospel is usually identified with the Mark mentioned in the epistles as the companion of both Peter and Paul, with the John Mark mentioned in the Acts of the Apostles, and possibly also the young man who is described running away when Jesus was arrested in Gethsemane.

According to tradition he was the son of the Mary who owned a house in Jerusalem and provided hospitality to the apostles. Although not one of Jesus' disciples himself, he later became a kind of spokesman for Peter, who writes of 'my son Mark'. But he is also mentioned as one of the companions of Paul on his first missionary journey and was with him again when he was a prisoner in Rome, where he probably wrote his Gospel.

There is a further tradition that he went to Alexandria to preach, became that city's bishop and was martyred there, and that in the ninth century his remains were brought from Alexandria to Venice, whose principal patron he has long been.

*St Luke, by the humanist scribe Peter Meghen (1466-1537)*

# Luke (18 October)

The author of the Gospel that bears his name and of the Acts of the Apostles was a Greek, possibly born in Antioch, and a physician by profession. His Gospel puts particular stress on Jesus' openness to Gentiles, to women, and to society's outcasts. From his account in Acts it is believed that he accompanied Paul on some of his missionary journeys, and from Paul's epistles we know that he was in Rome, where, Paul writes, 'Luke is my only companion'. Nothing else is known of his life, but a writer of the second or third century records that he died in Greece at the age of eighty-four.

Luke is the patron saint of physicians and surgeons, but also of painters, because of a legend that he painted portraits of the Blessed Virgin.

# John the Divine

(27 December)

By tradition the same John is the author of the fourth Gospel, three New Testament epistles and the book of Revelation. There is also a tradition that he was 'the disciple whom Jesus loved' and who leaned against His breast at the Last Supper, whom Jesus on the cross asked to care for His mother, and who first recognized the risen Christ by the Sea of Tiberias. He was, like his brother James, a Galilean fisherman, called away from his nets to follow Jesus. His Gospel is the most theological and spiritual of the four, but also contains historical detail absent from the other three.

He is mentioned in the Acts of the Apostles as the companion of Peter in his imprisonment, and Paul describes him as a pillar of the Christian community in Jerusalem. In later years he was exiled to the Greek island of Patmos 'because I had preached God's word and borne my testimony to Jesus', and it was there that he wrote his visionary Revelations. John is believed to have spent his last years at Ephesus and to have died there at a great age.

*Detail from The Four Apostles by Albrecht Dürer (1471-1528)*

# Barnabas (11 June)

Barnabas was a Jew from Cyprus who sold his estate and gave the proceeds to the community of followers of Jesus he joined in Jerusalem. Although not one of the twelve disciples of Jesus, he was called an apostle by the early fathers and was an important figure in the earliest days of Christianity. It was he who persuaded the persecuted followers of Jesus to accept Paul, their former persecutor, after his conversion. When the church sent him to Antioch to give guidance to the converts there, he brought Paul from Tarsus to help him, and in fact it was at Antioch that the term 'Christian' was first used.

He accompanied Paul and John Mark on the first overseas mission, to Cyprus, his birthplace, and was, with Paul, among the first to preach to the Gentiles. In a famous incident the pagans at Iconium, in Lycaonia, mistook Paul for the god Mercury and Barnabas for Jupiter and had to be restrained from offering sacrifices to them. Later the two men had a falling-out, and nothing more is heard of Barnabas in the New Testament after he is recorded as setting off again for Cyprus with John Mark. He is said to have been martyred by stoning to death at Salamis, the Cypriot port, around the year 60.

*The Miracle of St Barnabas, by Veronese (1528–88)*

*Stoning of St Stephen by Gentile da Fabriano (c.1370-1427)*

# Stephen (26 December)

The first Christian martyr was a Greek-speaking Jew who was chosen to be one of the seven deacons appointed by the apostles to look after the needs of Greek-speaking widows in the Christian community of Jerusalem. He was also a preacher who 'did great wonders and miracles', but he had made enemies who conspired against him and denounced him to the Jewish council. Summoned to answer the charge that he was a blasphemer, he denounced the council at length, describing them as men who resisted the Holy Spirit and had killed the Righteous One foretold by the prophets. He was taken out of the city and stoned to death. His dying words were 'Lord, lay not this sin to their charge!' Holding the coats of the men who stoned him was a young man from Tarsus, by name Saul, later to become Paul.

# Paul (29 June)

'The apostle to the Gentiles' before his conversion was named Saul. He was a Jew from Tarsus who had inherited Roman citizenship from his father and was brought up as a strict Pharisee. As a young man in Jerusalem he devoted himself to the persecution of the Christians, helping to seek them out and hand them over to the authorities for imprisonment and even death. Then, while on a journey to Damascus to conduct persecutions there, he was thrown from his horse and had a vision in which Jesus Christ rebuked him and told him that it was his destiny to take the Gospel to the Gentiles. Saul, now calling himself by the Greek name Paul, was baptized. After some years in Damascus, in Jerusalem and at Antioch he began his great missionary journeys in about the year 45.

He travelled first to Cyprus and then widely around the countries of the eastern Mediterranean, including Greece: 'In journeyings often, in perils of waters, in perils of robbers, in perils by mine own countrymen, in perils by the heathen, in perils in the city, in perils in the wilderness, in perils in the sea, in perils among false brethren; in weariness and painfulness, in watchings often, in hunger and thirst, in fastings often, in cold and nakedness'. These journeys lasted for about twelve years, during which he preached, founded churches and then wrote letters to those new churches to guide them and keep them in the faith. Around the year 57 he was arrested in Jerusalem. Demanding his right to trial as a Roman citizen, he was eventually sent to Rome. There is some indication that he was acquitted at his first trial and spent some years at liberty, possibly travelling as far as Spain. But at some point he must have been re-arrested, brought again to Rome and there eventually executed. As a Roman citizen he was beheaded, not crucified.

He is described in a second century document as short, bald and bow-legged, unimpressive in physical appearance, but his letters reveal a man of mighty intellect, whose thought is second only to the recorded words of Jesus Himself in the development of the doctrines of Christianity.

29

*The Apostle Paul by Rembrandt (1606-69)*

# Polycarp (23 February)

Polycarp, bishop of Smyrna, was one of that small group of 'Apostolic Fathers' who received instruction directly from the apostles, in his case from St John the Evangelist. Little or nothing is known about his long life, save that he was an important figure among the churches of Asia Minor who travelled to Rome to confer with the pope of that day, but a written record of his martyrdom survives.

During the persecutions of the emperor Marcus Aurelius, in the year 155, he was betrayed by a slave and arrested at a villa outside Smyrna where he was taking refuge. He was brought into the city and called upon by the proconsul, before a hostile crowd in the games stadium, to take an oath by the guardian spirit of the emperor and to curse Christ. Polycarp replied, 'Fourscore and six years have I served Him and He hath done me no wrong. How then can I blaspheme my King and Saviour?' While he continued to confess his faith, the crowd clamoured for the blood of the man 'who destroys our gods'. The proconsul at length ordered him to be burnt to death. Polycarp welcomed death, refusing to be tied to the stake. When the fire was lit, 'the flames made a kind of arch, like a ship's sail filled with the wind...and he looked, not like burning flesh, but like bread in the oven or gold and silver being refined in the furnace'. At last, the order was given to kill him with a spear and his body was placed in the middle of the fire and burnt to ashes lest his followers worship his remains.

# Concordius (1 January)

This early Roman martyr spent most of his adult life in solitary prayer and meditation. About 178, during the emperor Marcus Aurelius's persecution of the Christians, he was brought before Torquatus, governor of Umbria, and promised release if he would worship a statue of Jupiter. When he refused he was beaten, tortured on the rack and confined in a death cell. Given one last chance to honour an image of one of the Roman gods, he spat at it, and was promptly beheaded.

# Cecilia (22 November)

C ecilia may have lived in Rome in the second or third century. According to her legend she was a young Christian woman of patrician rank who was betrothed against her will to a pagan named Valerian. On their wedding night she requested him to respect her vow that she would remain a virgin. Valerian was so impressed by her Christian faith and serenity that he was baptized, along with his brother, Tiburtius. Eventually the two men were arrested and taken before the Roman prefect; refusing to honour the pagan gods, they were put to death, along with one of the prefect's officers, Maximus, who had been so moved by their calm demeanour that he was converted to Christianity.

Cecilia herself was brought before the prefect and sentenced to death by suffocation in her own bathroom. Her executioners stoked the fires of the hypocaust till the steam was scalding but she remained unscathed. Then one of them was ordered to strike off her head. He hacked at her neck three times, but failed to kill her, and she lingered in pain for three days before she died.

Cecilia is the patroness of musicians, because a sixth century account of her martyrdom speaks of her singing to God 'in her heart' and of there being musicians at her wedding.

Detail from: *St Cecilia, by John Melhuish Strudwick (1849-1937)*

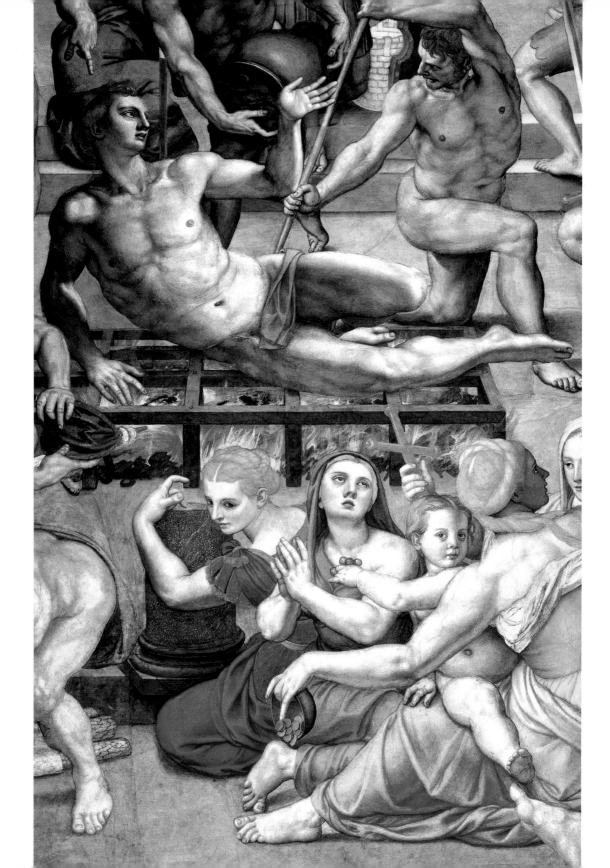

# Valentine (14 February)

Valentine is the name of a Christian martyr of the third century. Except that he was a bishop almost nothing else is known about him. The connection of his name with the modern custom of sending 'valentine' cards to chosen lovers is probably due either to the coincidence of his feast-day with the start of the Roman fertility festival of Lupercalia or with the old tradition that it was the date of the beginning of the mating season for birds.

*St Lawrence, Anon, Mausoleum Galla Placidia, Ravenna (5th century)*

# Lawrence (10 August)

According to tradition, Lawrence was a deacon of the church in Rome in the service of Pope Sixtus II during the persecutions of the third century emperor Valerian. When Sixtus himself went to his martyrdom in 258, Lawrence accompanied him, asking why he should die rather than his deacon. Sixtus replied, 'My son, I am not leaving you. In three days you will follow me'.

The prefect of Rome then ordered Lawrence to hand over all the wealth of the church. Lawrence, confident that he was about to go to his death, assembled thousands of the poor, the sick and the aged and presented them to the prefect, saying, 'These are the church's treasure'. The prefect, enraged, ordered him to be put to death by roasting on a heated gridiron. That is the tradition, which made him one of the most revered martyrs of the city of Rome. In historical fact he was probably beheaded.

*The Martyrdom of St Lawrence, by Agnolo Bronzino (1503-72)*

# Antony the Abbot (17 January)

St Antony is regarded as the founder of monasticism, although he himself spent most of his life in solitude as a hermit.

He was born in 251 in a village near Memphis in Egypt. On the death of his parents, who were Christians, he found himself a wealthy man. When he was about twenty, however, inspired by the words of Jesus Christ to another rich young man, he sold most of what he possessed and distributed the price he received among the poor. Then he retired into desert solitude, overcoming the temptations of Satan, acquiring a reputation for great spiritual wisdom and attracting many followers. The monasteries he founded for those followers when in his fifties were loose communities of individual hermits, whom he visited occasionally.

On two occasions he travelled to Alexandria, to defend the Christians there against persecution and to preach against the Arian heresy, having acquired by then such fame that the emperor Constantine wrote to him asking for his prayers. But for the most part he lived alone, in increasingly remote places, spending his days in prayer and meditation and in the simple manual work necessary for his survival. He died peacefully in 356, one hundred and five years old.

*St Antony the Abbot, French School (15th century)*

# Helen (18 August)

The mother of the emperor Constantine the Great was born c.255, probably at Drepanum in Bithynia, possibly the daughter of an inn-keeper. She met and married the Roman general Constantius Chlorus and bore him a son, Constantine in 274, but on becoming emperor in 293 Constantius repudiated her for political reasons and married in her place Theodora, daughter of the emperor Maximian. It is not known for certain when she became a Christian, but when, in 306, Constantine succeeded his father, he honoured her greatly. In 312, after entering Rome and declaring Christianity a tolerated religion, he conferred on her the titles Augusta and 'Nobilissima Femina', re-named her birthplace Helenopolis and struck coins bearing her image. She devoted herself to the promotion of the Christian religion, endowing and enriching many churches, helping the poor, and herself living humbly and dressing modestly.

In 324, in old age, she went to the Holy Land, continuing her work there and supervising the building of a great church on the site of Golgotha and the holy sepulchre, after the removal of a temple to Venus which the emperor Hadrian had erected there. It is here, according to tradition, that she found the cross on which Jesus Christ was crucified. Such a discovery was claimed at the time, and although it was not until 395 that St Ambrose identified her with it, her name has ever since been associated with the true cross. She died, possibly in Palestine, c.330 and her remains were taken to Rome.

*St Helen, British (15th century)*

# Athanasius (2 May)

The great doctor of the Church who has been called 'the Champion of Orthodoxy' and whose name is associated with the Athanasian Creed was born c.297 at Alexandria, whose bishop he became in 328. As a deacon he was present at the Council of Nicea in 325, called by the emperor Constantine to establish the tenets of orthodox Christian belief. The Council denounced the teachings of bishop Arius, who held that Jesus Christ was created in time by God, not begotten, and was not truly part of the Godhead. Arius was expelled, along with several of his followers, but his teaching spread rapidly around the Mediterranean and was supported by many of the clergy and by some of the emperors who succeeded Constantine.

Athanasius spent a large part of his life defending orthodoxy against the Arian heresy, at a time when religious controversy caused violent disputes among ordinary citizens, often leading to death. For long periods he was himself driven out of his bishopric when the Arians brought false accusations of theft, sacrilege, sedition and even murder against him and he found himself at risk of losing his liberty and even his life. In all he spent seventeen years in exile, many of them in the Egyptian desert, where he was protected by the hermit communities. In 366, after the death of the emperor Julian the Apostate, he was welcomed back to Alexandria, where he spent the last seven years of his life in relative peace and safety.

Athanasius wrote much throughout his lifetime, including a life of St Antony, but he was not the author of the Athanasian Creed, although it may well have been based on his written and spoken thoughts.

# Sebastian (20 January)

According to the legend, Sebastian was a Roman soldier, born in Gaul, and a secret Christian at a time in the early fourth century when they were being persecuted by the emperor Diocletian. His military abilities came to the notice of the emperor, who made him an officer in his praetorian guard. When Sebastian's faith became known, Diocletian was enraged and ordered him to be shot to death with arrows, an ordeal which made him a popular subject with Renaissance artists. He survived this, however, and was nursed back to health by Irene, the widow of another Christian martyr. On learning of this, Diocletian sentenced him to be beaten to death with cudgels. His body was then flung into a sewer, but his fellow Christians managed to rescue it and buried it on the Appian Way, where the church of San Sebastiano now stands.

*Detail from St George by Giovanni Bellini (1430-1516)*

# George (23 April)

The patron saint of England is thought to have been a Roman soldier from Cappadocia, who was martyred, probably in Palestine, in the early years of the fourth century. The story is that he was tortured and executed during the persecutions of Diocletian after tearing down an imperial edict ordering Christians to make sacrifices to the gods of Rome. The legend of his killing a dragon to save the life of a maiden is a later medieval addition.

Although his name and legend were known in the British Isles before the Norman Conquest, it is likely that his fame there was spread by crusaders returning from Palestine, which was the centre of his cult. His emblem, of a red cross on a white field, certainly suggests a link with the crusades. It is probable, though not certain, that he became England's patron saint when King Edward III founded the Order of the Garter in the mid-fourteenth century.

*St Sebastian by Antonio Pollaiuolo (1432/3-98)*

# Nicholas (6 December)

The saint long-associated with Christmas under the name Santa Claus (from the Dutch dialect form, Sinte Klaas) was a bishop in Myra in south-west Asia Minor in the fourth century. Nothing else is known for certain about his life, but countless legends surround him, including miracles, acts of great charity, and the rescue of seamen. He was famous enough in his day for the emperor Justinian to build a church in his honour at Constantinople in the sixth century.

He is the patron saint of children, sailors and pawnbrokers (his emblem is three gold balls) and of many cities and countries.

# John of Egypt (27 March)

This John was born at Lycopolis in Egypt c.300 and worked as a carpenter until, at the age of twenty-five, he gave up the world to become a hermit. When he was about forty he went to a hill near Lycopolis and there carved out for himself a set of three little cells: a bedroom, a work-room and an oratory. Then he walled himself in for the remainder of his days, leaving only one small window through which he received food and water and spoke to visitors. Henceforth he ate only dried fruit and vegetables, but on this diet he lived for another fifty years.

For five days of the week he lived in absolute solitude, but on Saturdays and Sundays men were permitted to approach his window. He won a reputation for miracles, for prophecy, and for his ability to read minds. Oil blessed by him effected remarkable cures. Visitors became so numerous that a hospice had to be built nearby to accommodate them. Foreseeing his own death at the age of ninety, he closed his window and commanded that no-one should come near for three days. His body was found kneeling in prayer.

Previous page: *St Nicholas rebuking the Tempest by Bicci di Lorenzo (1375-1452)*

# Elmo (Erasmus)

(2 June)

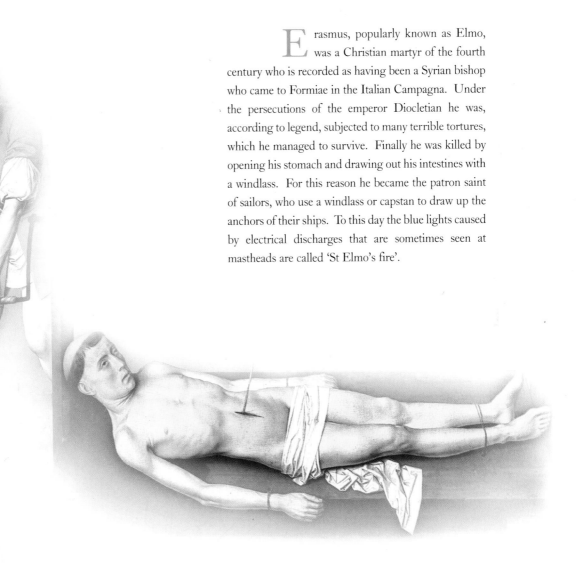

E rasmus, popularly known as Elmo, was a Christian martyr of the fourth century who is recorded as having been a Syrian bishop who came to Formiae in the Italian Campagna. Under the persecutions of the emperor Diocletian he was, according to legend, subjected to many terrible tortures, which he managed to survive. Finally he was killed by opening his stomach and drawing out his intestines with a windlass. For this reason he became the patron saint of sailors, who use a windlass or capstan to draw up the anchors of their ships. To this day the blue lights caused by electrical discharges that are sometimes seen at mastheads are called 'St Elmo's fire'.

*Above and next page: Martyrdom of St Erasmus by Dieric Bouts (1410/20-75)*

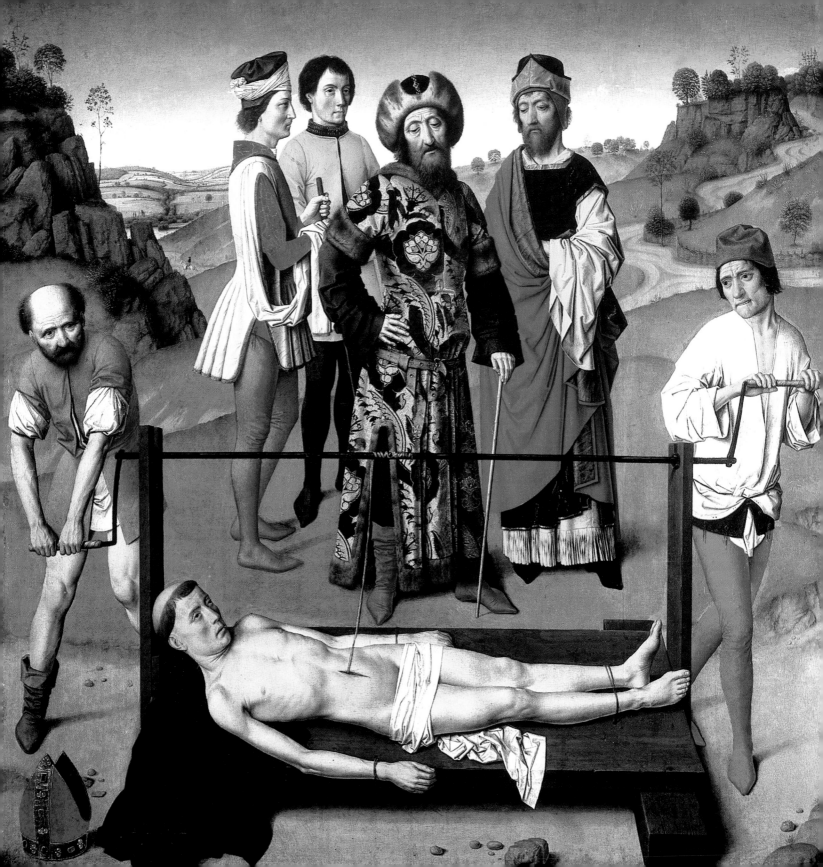

# Ambrose (7 December)

A mbrose was born at Trier in 340, the son of a high Roman official in Gaul. He trained as a lawyer, and in c.370 was appointed governor of the province of Aemilia and Liguria, whose capital was at Milan. In 374 he was chosen to be bishop of Milan by popular acclamation, although he was still under instruction as a Christian and not yet baptized. Thereafter he devoted himself to study of the scriptures and lived a life of great simplicity and humility, giving away his possessions and washing the feet of new Christian converts, despite the fact that this was not the Roman custom.

At this period Milan was effectively the capital of the western Roman empire, and Christian bishops were powerful figures in the secular as well as the spiritual world. Paganism was still widespread, and many Christians were adherents of the Arian heresy. When a group of pagan senators tried to restore a statue of the goddess of Victory to the senate-house in Rome, Ambrose was able to intervene successfully with the young emperor Valentinian II to have this stopped. When he was ordered by the empress-regent, Justina, to hand over one of his churches to the Arians, he refused. In 390 the emperor of the east, Theodosius I, ordered a massacre of the citizens of Thessaloniki in reprisal for riots in which the Roman governor had been killed. Ambrose wrote to him demanding that he do public penance for this act; the emperor submitted and did so. As Ambrose put it: 'The emperor is within the Church; he is not above it'.

In his role as bishop Ambrose was a great popular preacher, who also made extensive use of hymns. In the history of the Christian Church, he is perhaps most famous for the fact that in 387 he baptized Augustine. He is one of the four great Latin doctors of the Church, along with Augustine, Jerome and Gregory the Great.

Detail from: *St Ambrose by Simone Martini (1280-1344)*

# Basil the Great

(2 January)

One of the doctors of the Church, Basil was born in Caesarea around 330 but studied in Athens, where he showed great brilliance. After lecturing at the university for a time, he adopted the life of a hermit in remote Pontus, but so many people gathered around him there to receive his teaching that he was obliged to found a monastery. The rules he established for men who wished to live together as monks are still the basis of monastic rule in Eastern Christendom.

Persuaded after five years to return to city life so that his preaching could convert multitudes of unbelievers, he became Archbishop of Caesarea, where he gave away his personal possessions and built a hospital for the poor. At odds with the Roman state, he was threatened at one time with exile, torture and death. As for exile, he replied, it was no threat, since he lived already as a stranger on this earth, travelling towards the kingdom of God. As for torture, 'only the first blow will hurt me. As for death, that will benefit me, bringing me even closer to my God for whom I completely live'. He was left alone, and died peacefully in 379.

*St Basil, Chrysostom and Gregory (18th century)*

# Jerome (30 September)

The great father of the Church and biblical scholar was born to Christian parents in Dalmatia c.342. He studied in Rome and spent several years among the hermit communities of Syria, where he learned Hebrew from a rabbi, before continuing his studies in Constantinople. He was, reluctantly, ordained a priest at Antioch, but never exercised the priestly office, preferring the life of a monk. In 382 he became secretary to Pope Damasus in Rome, and it was then that he began work on revising the existing Latin translation of the New Testament and the psalms, a project which eventually became the complete Latin Bible, largely translated by him, known since the middle ages as the Vulgate; it was completed in c.404.

At Rome also he became the leader of a group of devout and wealthy women, including (Saint) Paula, her daughter (Saint) Eustochium, and another named Marcella. When, following the death of Damasus, he decided to return to the East, they followed him. In 386 they settled in Bethlehem, where Paula used some of her wealth to build communal dwellings for both men and women wishing to live the religious life, as well as a hospice for pilgrims and a school, at which Jerome taught.

Apart from his biblical scholarship, Jerome engaged in the religious controversies of his day, writing with a virulence which won him many enemies. He seems to have had a violent temper, and treated his opponents with savage contempt, but his friends and followers held him in great affection and he performed many acts of kindness to the poor and weak. He died in Bethlehem in 420. Jerome is the patron saint of librarians.

Detail from: *St Jerome in his Study, by Domenico Ghirlandaio (1449-94)*

# John Chrysostom (13 September)

John was born at Antioch c.347, the son of a senior officer in the Roman army, and was brought up as a Christian by his mother. After training as a lawyer he became a hermit for some years, enduring a regime of asceticism which may have permanently impaired his health. Then in 381 he returned to Antioch, where he gained a reputation as a miraculously gifted preacher who could expound Scripture with extraordinary vividness and immediacy; hence the name he acquired: Chrysostom, 'Golden Mouth'. In 398, against his wishes, he became patriarch of Constantinople, and in that capacity began a campaign of reform, social and ecclesiastical, which attracted the enmity both of the rich and powerful and of fellow churchmen; in particular, Eudoxia, the emperor's wife, and Theophilus, patriarch of Alexandria, became his enemies. In 403 they succeeded in having him deposed on trumped-up charges and sent into exile in Armenia, from where he wrote many letters describing the hardships he endured. In Constantinople his supporters strove to bring about his return, but in 407 he died of exhaustion during a march into an even more remote place of exile.

John is recognized as one of the four great Greek doctors of the Church.

*Saints Gregory, St Chrysostom and Basil the Great, Byzantine*

*St Augustine by El Greco (1541-1614)*

# Augustine (28 August)

Augustine was born in 354 in what is now Algeria. His father was a pagan, but his mother, (Saint) Monica, was a Christian and raised her son in that religion, although he did not seek baptism. At the age of sixteen he went to Carthage to study rhetoric and there took a mistress, who bore him a son, Adeodatus, to whom he was devoted. Deeply engaged in philosophy, and not yet a convinced Christian, he was drawn for a time to the dualist teachings of Manichaeism. In 383 he went to Rome, and then to Milan, where his mother, anxious for the state of his soul, followed him. Both mother and son came under the influence of Ambrose, then bishop of Milan. Augustine went through a period of spiritual and intellectual torment, torn between the pleasures of the world and the flesh and the prospect of a life devoted to God. It ended one day in 386 when he was sitting in a garden and heard a voice, like that of a child, saying 'Tolle, lege. Tolle, lege', 'Take and read'. He took up the copy of St Paul's epistles that a friend had been reading and opened it. The words he read convinced him at last and he was baptized, along with his son, on Easter eve, 387. Monica greatly rejoiced that her son had become a Christian. She died not long afterwards, and is now venerated as a saint, with her feast-day on 27 August.

In 388 Augustine returned to Africa, where he led a life of fasting, prayer, meditation, teaching and charitable works, but in 391, against his wishes, he was ordained a priest and in 395 he was consecrated bishop of Hippo, where he was to spend the remaining thirty-four years of his life, the dominant figure in the Christian world. He insisted that his cathedral clergy live in community with him, under strict monastic rule, renouncing all personal property. He spent his days teaching, preaching, caring for his community and for the poor, administering justice in the city, arguing against the powerful heresies of the day, constantly writing. His written output was formidable, including more than one hundred books and treatises, 200 letters, 500 sermons. Two of his books are still read today: his remarkable autobiography, *Confessions,* and *The City of God,* occasioned by the sacking of Rome by the Goths in 410, although not completed until 426. He died in August 430, as the Vandals were besieging his own city of Hippo.

Detail from: *St Augustine by Fra Filippo Lippi (1406-69)*

# Patrick (17 March)

The patron saint of Ireland was a Romano-Briton, born c.385 somewhere on the west coast of Britain. His father was a Roman official, his grandfather a Christian priest. At about the age of sixteen he was captured by raiders and taken into slavery in pagan Ireland. There, while he was employed as a herdsman, near Ballymena in Antrim, he became deeply religious and prayed constantly to God.

After six years he managed to escape on a ship bound for Gaul, but at some time after gaining his freedom he was called in a dream to return to Ireland and preach the Gospel. According to tradition, he was trained for the priesthood in Gaul, under St Germanus of Auxerre, and in the year 432 he returned to the place of his captivity as a missionary bishop.

There were Christians in Ireland before his arrival, but they had made little impression. Patrick's preaching was extremely successful, and it was he who brought an organized Irish church into existence. At Tara in Meath he confronted the high-king, Laoghaire, silenced the druids, and won an audience for the Gospel of Christ; the king's daughters were among his many converts. In 444 he established his episcopal see at Armagh, by which time he had the help of several other bishops and numerous lesser clergy. He died in 461 at Saul on Strangford Lough. His surviving writings include his Confession and the hymn called Lorica, 'the Breastplate'.

# Simeon Stylites (5 January)

Simeon was born near Aleppo in Syria around 390. Growing up as a simple shepherd boy, he was early drawn to the idea of enlightenment through suffering and while still in his teens entered a monastery as a servant. After two years he joined another where the rule was stricter and where he came near to death through fasting. Expelled from the monastery for his extreme asceticism, he became a hermit and was soon drawing crowds attracted by his reputation as a worker of miracles.

In 423, by now famous, he began living at the top of a pillar (hence his name, from the Greek word *stylos*) in order to find the seclusion he needed for meditation. This was at first six feet high, but in time was extended to more than fifty feet. At its top, perhaps five feet in diameter, he lived completely exposed to the elements, nourished by small gifts of food from disciples and descending from time to time to give spiritual counsel and to relieve the sick. In all he lived in this manner for thirty-seven years, by his example converting many pagans to Christianity.

*Miracle of St Patrick, by Giovanni Battista Tiepolo (1696-1770)*

# Leo the Great (10 November)

Pope Leo I was born in Rome, but was probably a Tuscan. He succeeded to the papacy in 440 and before long was confronted with a doctrinal dispute over the nature of Christ. A monk named Eutyches had argued heretically that Christ had a single nature, his human side having been wholly subsumed by his divinity. A council of bishops was held at Chalcedon in 451 to debate the matter. Leo was not present in person, but a letter from him, known as 'the Tome', arguing for the orthodox position that Christ was both God and man, persuaded the assembly to confirm that view.

Leo's activities were not confined to the world of doctrine. In 452, when the Huns had invaded northern Italy and were threatening Rome, he went out and confronted Attila, their leader, and persuaded him to withdraw and to accept an annual tribute in return for ceasing his destruction of Roman cities. In 455 Leo failed to stop the Vandals occupying Rome but did succeed in obtaining their agreement merely to loot the city and to abstain from burning its buildings and massacring the citizens.

Leo also extended the authority of the papacy over most of the Western Empire, while restraining the influence of the patriarchate of Constantinople.

He died in 461 and was declared to be a doctor of the Church in 1754.

# Hilary (5 May)

Hilary, who became bishop of Arles, was born c.440 into a noble family. He was groomed from boyhood for the religious life by his predecessor, St Honoratus, who was a close relative, and succeeded him when he was barely thirty years of age. As bishop he was twice censured by Pope Leo I for exceeding his episcopal authority, but after his death in 449 the same pope described him as 'Hilary of blessed memory'.

*St Simeon, Russian School (16th century)*

# Brigid (1 February)

Little is known about the Irish saint known as 'the Mary of the Gael' save that she founded at Kildare the first women's religious community in Ireland. She was born c.450, probably the daughter of a chief, and became a nun while still in her teens. The tales surrounding her life speak of her concern for the material and spiritual welfare of the poor and of her many acts of charity, some of them associated with miracles. As abbess of Kildare she presided over a centre of learning, where books were copied and illuminated. According to legend, during a synod of the Irish church, one of the fathers announced that he had had a dream foretelling that the Holy Mother would appear among them. When Brigid arrived, he cried out, 'There is the holy maiden I saw in my dream'; since when she has been known as 'the Mary of the Gael'.

She died at Kildare c.525 and was buried there, but when the Danes invaded, her body was moved to Downpatrick, to lie beside the remains of St Patrick, her fellow patron saint of Ireland.

*Detail from St Brigid, Danish (12th century)*

# Benedict (11 July)

The author of the fundamental rule of western monasticism was born into a noble family in Nursia (Norcia) in Umbria in c.480. He was educated in Rome, but at about the age of twenty, revolted by the immorality of the city, he adopted the life of a recluse at Subiaco, from where, over the years, he established several small monasteries for the disciples who flocked to him because of his reputation for sanctity and wisdom; by tradition there were twelve of these monasteries, each with twelve monks. Then, c.530, Benedict founded the monastery principally associated with him, at Monte Cassino, between Rome and Naples, on the site of a former pagan temple. He died peacefully in his monastery c.547, standing erect, supported by his monks, and saying his last prayers.

It was almost certainly at Monte Cassino that he drew up his Rule for the conduct of monastic communities, 'a school of the Lord's service, in which we hope to order nothing harsh or rigorous'. Disciplined, but humane, and essentially sensible and practical, allowing for different individual capabilities, it remains to this day the basis for the regulation of daily life in monasteries of the Western Church throughout the world.

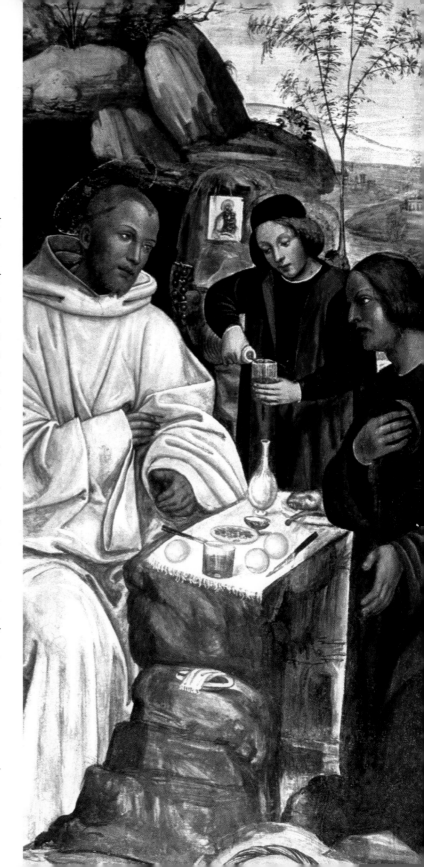

*St Benedict against a Landscape,*
*by Signorelli (c.1441-1523)*

M. Canaria.

Insulæ Fortunatæ.

Cabo Finis terræ

Hispan

Babaria

Cabo de No:

M. Attlas

Africa.

# Brendan (16 May)

The great Irish monk and traveller was born in Kerry c.486. As a child he was brought up in the care of the abbess (Saint) Ita, who ran a school for small boys as part of her community, and in due time became a priest and a monk. In the course of his long life he founded several monasteries, of which the most famous is Clonfert, said to have housed three thousand monks. He is known as 'Brendan the Voyager' from the many seaborne journeys he is reputed to have made in his skin-covered coracle. These took him to the west coast of Britain, perhaps to Brittany, and according to a tenth century tale which spread throughout Christendom, far out into the Atlantic, perhaps as far as Greenland, or even North America. He died in 578.

# Germanus of Paris (28 May)

Germanus was born near Autun c.496 and was abbot of the monastery of St Symphorian there when the see of Paris became vacant and, happening to be in the city at the time, he was appointed to it by the Frankish king Childebert I in c.556. He also became Childebert's chaplain and was greatly influential in returning the king to a more Christian way of life. In 558 Childebert founded the great abbey which Germanus consecrated to St Vincent and the Holy Cross and which after his death was re-named Saint-Germain-des-Prés. He was less successful, however, in his efforts to curb the brutal and licentious ways of the Frankish nobility and to put an end to the savage fratricidal wars that broke out among Childebert's successors. Throughout his life he retained a monk's simplicity of life and was constant in his generosity to the city's poor. He was greatly mourned when he died in 576 and was buried in the church of the abbey that later bore his name.

*Previous page: St Brendan and his crew on a whale (British Library MS)*

*St Brendan, by Edward Reginald Frampton (1872-1923)*

# Columba (9 June)

Columba was born in Donegal c.520, and trained for the priesthood from an early age. After his ordination he spent some fifteen years preaching in his native Ireland, where he also founded monasteries, notably at Derry and Durrow. Then, probably in the year 563, he left his country and, with twelve companion monks, settled on the island of Iona, off the west coast of the much larger island of Mull. There he founded a monastery. At this time, at least some of the Irish who had settled in Argyll were Christian, but the Picts of what is now called Scotland were still heathen, and it was to them that he directed his first missions. During the thirty-four years that remained to him he travelled extensively on the Scottish mainland and is credited with many miracles, including the driving away of a monster from Loch Ness by means of the sign of the cross, which is believed to have assisted in the conversion of the Pictish king Brude and many of his people. Columba also founded other monasteries which, from Iona, carried the Celtic form of Christianity south into Northern England.

*St Columba, Anon, Oak Grove, Ireland*

# David (1 March)

David, in Welsh Dewi, patron saint of Wales, was born c.520, the son, according to his legend, of Sant, a chieftain of Ceredigion (Cardigan) and of Saint Non.

His principal monastery was at Mynyw (now St David's) in Pembrokeshire. There he and his monks led an austere life of constant prayer and hard labour, speaking only when strictly necessary, eating only bread and vegetables and drinking only water and a little milk. According to an eleventh century biography, he founded twelve monasteries, went on pilgrimage to Jerusalem, where he was consecrated bishop, and eventually became primate of Wales, at which time he moved the episcopal see from Caerleon to Mynyw. There he taught many later Welsh saints, and there, perhaps in 589, he died.

# Illtyd (6 November)

Little is known for certain about the sixth century Welsh saint, save that he was famous in his own day and that he was active chiefly in the south-east of the country. The early seventh century Life of St Samson states that he was ordained by St Germanus of Paris, that he was greatly learned, and that he presided over a great monastery school at Llanilltyd Fawr (Llantwit Major) in Glamorgan, where Samson himself was a pupil.

# Gregory the Great (3 September)

The great pope, statesman and doctor of the Church was born in Rome c.540. His family was patrician, and he himself served in the civilian administration, rising to the office of prefect of Rome, before becoming a monk in c.575. From 579 until 585 he was papal agent at Constantinople. Then, in 590, he was elected pope, the first monk to hold that office.

His pontificate lasted until his death in 604. These were years of danger and difficulty throughout Christian Europe, when the Germanic tribes were either threatening or already occupying much of what had been the western Roman Empire. Gregory negotiated with the Lombards in northern Italy and with the Franks and Visigoths in France and Spain. He devoted the wealth of the Church to relieving the victims of war, plague and famine and to ransoming prisoners. He sent Augustine to convert the Anglo-Saxons in Britain, inspired, it is said, by the sight of fair-haired Saxon youths in the Roman slave-market, and took a great interest in this mission.

Aside from his diplomatic and administrative activities, he was a prolific writer. His writings include, notably, a book of rules for the conduct of a bishop, a commentary on the book of Job, and accounts of the lives of Italian saints. Over 800 of his letters have survived. He also reformed the worship of the Church and introduced what is now called Gregorian chant. Although a man of immense power and influence in his time, it was he who described the office of pope as to be 'the servant of the servants of God'.

*Pope Gregory the Great by Carlo Saraceni (c.1580-1620)*

# Columban (23 November)

The greatest of the Irish missionaries to continental Europe was born in Leinster c.540. He became a monk while still a youth and for many years was at the great monastery of Bangor in Ulster. When he was about forty-five he obtained his abbot's permission to leave the monastery and travel abroad with twelve companions, who included (Saint) Gall. He founded monastic centres at Annegray, Luxeuil and Fontaine in the Vosges, under the patronage of the king of Burgundy, while his followers founded numerous others in France, Germany, Switzerland and Italy.

After some time the severity of Columban's rule and his adherence to Celtic customs, for example in the dating of Easter, brought him into conflict with the Frankish bishops, and he was obliged to defend himself in letters to the pope. Then he incurred the enmity of Brunhilda, grandmother of the young King Theodoric II of Burgundy, by rebuking him for loose living and by denying her admission to his monastery. In 610 he and his Irish brethren were ordered to be deported to Ireland. Instead of returning there, however, Columban and some of his companions travelled to Lake Constance, where they lived for about two years, before moving over the Alps into Lombardy. There he vehemently opposed the Arianism of Agilulf, king of the Lombards, but the king nonetheless gave him land at Bobbio, between Genoa and Piacenza. There, in 614, he began the establishment of his famous abbey, doing much of the work himself, though then in his seventies. He died at Bobbio the following year.

# Aidan (31 August)

Aidan, who played such a great part in the conversion of northern England, was born in Ireland, and was a monk at Iona when, around 635, he was requested by King Oswald to bring missionaries to Northumberland. He became bishop and settled on the island of Lindisfarne, where, with the support of the king, he built a monastery. There he trained English boys to teach the faith to their countrymen, and from there he himself travelled far and wide on his missionary journeys.

The death of Oswald in battle in 642 was a great blow to him. He was equally devoted to Oswald's successor, his cousin Oswin. When Oswin in turn was killed in 651, Aidan died less than a fortnight later, from grief it is believed.

# Augustine of Canterbury (27 May)

In 596 Pope Gregory the Great sent Augustine, who was then prior of the monastery of St Andrew in Rome, along with forty of his monks, to preach to the Anglo-Saxons who now controlled most of Southern Britain but were still heathen. Despite their fears of working among a people reputed to be fierce and barbarous they landed in Kent in 597 and were welcomed by the local king, Ethelbert, whose Frankish wife was already a Christian. Ethelbert himself soon converted to Christianity along with many of his people. Augustine went at once to France, where he was consecrated archbishop of the English. He established his see at Canterbury, where he also founded the monastery of Saints Peter and Paul (re-named St Augustine's after his death). Later he established other sees at London and Rochester. He continued to work among the English until his death in c.605, but his influence probably did not extend much beyond the south-east of the country. Although he had sought their help, the British bishops of the south-west and of what is now Wales refused to recognize his primacy or to amend their Celtic practices in accordance with the Roman tradition. His successors, however, completed the work of the conversion of the English.

# Oswald of Northumbria (9 August)

Oswald, who would become the Christian king of Northumbria, was born c.605. In 617 his father, King Ethelfrith, was killed by King Redwald of the East Angles, and Oswald and his brothers went into exile in the west of Scotland, where they became Christians and were baptized at Iona.

In 633 Oswald raised an army, defeated and slew the Welsh king Cadwallon, who had killed his brothers, and recovered the Northumbrian kingdom. Now king himself, he asked the monks of Iona to send missionaries to convert his people to Christianity. They were led by Aidan, and the two men became close friends. According to Bede, Aidan was not fluent in English, but Oswald had learned Gaelic during his exile, and 'it was delightful to see the king himself interpreting God's word to his thanes and chief men'.

Under Oswald's rule, Northumbria became for a time the dominant English kingdom; he himself married Cyneburga, daughter of Cynegils, the first Christian king of Wessex. But after only eight years Penda, the heathen king of Mercia, took up arms against him and he was killed at the battle of Maserfelth (possibly Oswestry) in 642. As he died, according to tradition, he asked for God's mercy on those, friend and enemy, who were dying around him.

# Adrian (9 January)

Adrian was born in North Africa and was abbot of Nerida, near Naples, when in 664 the pope decided that he was the right man to succeed as archbishop of Canterbury. Adrian twice declined the office, saying that he was not fitted for such a great dignity and at length recommended a monk named Theodore in his stead. The pope agreed, and Theodore accepted the post on condition that Adrian assist him in the work.

The two men travelled to England in 668. Adrian taught at the monastery school of Saints Peter and Paul (later St Augustine's) at Canterbury and led a life of exemplary holiness until his death in 710. Students came from all over the British isles to receive instruction in the scriptures and in ecclesiastical doctrine but also in law, astronomy and mathematics. Bede claims that some of them came to know Greek and Latin as well as they knew English.

# Adamnan (23 September)

The ninth abbot of Iona was born c.624 in Donegal. He became abbot in 679, but spent much of his time in Ireland, where he had some success in replacing the Celtic with the Roman custom in the calculation of the date of Easter and in other matters, having been converted to this view himself as a result of his visits to the monasteries of Northumbria; he failed, however, to persuade the monks of his own Iona to alter their customs, and may have been unpopular with them. He is most famous for his biography of his predecessor, St Columba. Another book of his, *On the Holy Places*, was based on notes taken from conversations with a Frankish bishop, Arculf, whose ship was blown ashore on Iona on his return from a visit to Palestine. Adamnan died on Iona in 704.

# Benedict, or Benet, Biscop (12 January)

Born around 628, Biscop was a nobleman at the court of King Oswy of Northumbria who, after travelling to Rome, became a monk at the great monastery of Lérins in the South of France, taking the name Benedict. In 669 he returned to England, where he was abbot of the monastery at Canterbury for two years. In 674, after some time in Rome, he founded a new monastery at Wearmouth in his native Northumbria, bringing masons and glaziers from France. Eight years later he founded its sister house at Jarrow, where the Venerable Bede was one of his pupils and benefited from the great library that Benedict assembled there. Until struck down with paralysis in 686 he continued to travel to Rome, after one visit bringing back with him the precentor of St Peter's to instruct his English monks in Gregorian chant.

He died in 690 after three years of suffering which he bore with exemplary fortitude.

# Wilfrid (12 October)

Wilfrid was born in Northumbria in 634, the son of a thane. He was educated at the monastery of Lindisfarne and later spent some years in Lyons and in Rome, where he became convinced of the rightness of Roman customs in matters such as the dating of Easter and the tonsure, as against the Celtic traditions that then prevailed in northern England. On his return he became abbot of the new monastery at Ripon and soon afterwards was ordained to the priesthood.

At the great synod of Whitby, held in 664 to decide questions that were dividing Christian Britain, he played the major part in securing victory for the Roman party. He became bishop of York in 669. When the archbishop of Canterbury, (Saint) Theodore, divided the see of York without his consent he went to Rome to appeal against the decision, the first Englishman to take a lawsuit to the Roman courts. On his way there he spent some months on a mission to the heathen Germans of Friesland.

In Rome Wilfrid won his case, but on his return to Northumbria was imprisoned for nine months by King Egfrith, whom he had earlier offended by helping his wife to leave him and become a nun. On his release Wilfrid went to Sussex and used this period of exile to evangelize the Southern Saxons, most of whom were still pagan at this time, with the support of their recently baptized king, Ethelwald. Wilfrid returned to the north of England in 686, after the death of Egfrith, but in 691 he was again banished and in 703 he was obliged to return to Rome for another appeal. In a compromise settlement he became bishop of Hexham, administering the see from his monastery of Ripon, where he had introduced the Benedictine Rule. He died in 709, while visiting a monastery he had founded at Oundle, Northamptonshire.

# Cuthbert (20 March)

C uthbert was born somewhere in Northumbria, around the year 635, and in his boyhood worked as a shepherd. Inspired by a visionary experience in his mid-teens, he resolved to follow the religious life, and eventually became a monk at Melrose Abbey on the River Tweed. From there he made long journeys, sometimes on horseback, sometimes on foot, throughout the countryside from Berwick in the east to Galloway in the west, keeping the spirit of Christianity alive through his preaching at a time when people were in danger of relapsing into paganism. In 664 he moved to Lindisfarne and continued the work southward into Northumberland and Durham. The Venerable Bede describes him as 'the child of god', with an angelic sweetness of nature which deeply affected those who heard him preach. In his lifetime he had a reputation as a miracle-worker who effected many cures, but also as a man of great wisdom and practical kindness.

Although constantly active among his flock, Cuthbert seems to have had a longing for the solitary life of prayer and meditation. In 676 he obtained permission from his bishop to remove himself to the tiny uninhabited island of Farne, where he lived for six years. Despite the rough sea crossing, so many came to visit him there that he was obliged to build a guest house. In 684 he was summoned to return to the mainland as bishop of Hexham. Reluctantly accepting the call, he was consecrated at York but arranged to exchange the see at Hexham for that of Lindisfarne, where for two years he resumed an active life of teaching, preaching and alms-giving. When he felt the approach of death, however, he returned to his beloved Farne. There he died, and his remains were taken to Lindisfarne. When the Vikings began to raid the coast in the ninth century, his remains were moved to Durham cathedral, where they were rediscovered in 1827.

*St Cuthbert after his election cures an earl's servant (British Library MS)*

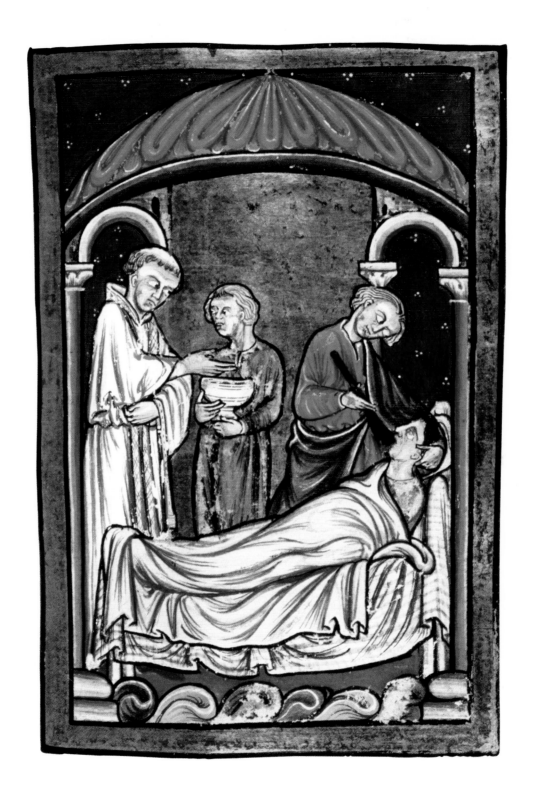

# Boniface (5 June)

The great missionary to the heathen Germans was born in Crediton, Devonshire, c.680, and was christened with the name Wynfrith. He was a monk in England for many years before he went to Germany in the year 718. His mission ranged widely over the still-pagan parts of that country and he made many lasting conversions and founded several monasteries. He never returned to his homeland, but he made three trips to Rome to report the progress of his work. In 732 the pope made him archbishop and he worked with King Pepin the Short to reform the Frankish church.

When he was in his early seventies he moved on to what is now called Holland and in c.755 met there a martyr's death, when he and his companions were attacked by heathens. Many letters by and about him survive, and reveal a man of deeply lovable character. St Cuthbert wrote of him, 'we in England reckon Boniface among the best and greatest teachers of the faith'.

*St Boniface by Alfred Rethel (1816-59)*

# Cyril and Methodius (14 February)

The two brothers known as 'the apostles of the Southern Slavs' are celebrated on the same day. Natives of Thessalonika, both rose to early prominence in the world of the Byzantine Empire: Cyril, born c.827, taught at the university of Constantinople, while his older brother Methodius was governor of a province in the Slav regions.

In 861 the two brothers were sent by the Emperor on a mission to convert the Khazars, in which they had considerable success. Returning to Constantinople, they were sent to teach the Gospel in heathen Moravia. In this they were greatly helped by their knowledge of the Slavonic language, and to aid them in the work Cyril developed an alphabet, known as the 'glagolithic' alphabet, in which it might be written down. The 'cyrillic' characters derived from Greek capital letters and used for Russian and other Slav languages today may also have been developed by Cyril but are more likely to have been the work of his followers.

In Moravia, the brothers were inhibited in their work by the hostility of the German clergy, who objected to their liturgical use of the Slav vernacular and to the fact that they were protegés of the Eastern Church. Among other difficulties, they were unable to ordain Moravian priests to aid them. Seeking help at the highest level, they went to Rome, where Pope Adrian II, after listening to their case, agreed to make both bishops. Sadly, Cyril died, in February 869, before he could be consecrated. Methodius, however, returned to the Slav lands. Despite the support of Rome, he continued to encounter difficulties from the German prelates and was even imprisoned for two years before Pope John VIII secured his release. Summoned to Rome in 879, he again successfully defended himself and was confirmed as archbishop of Moravia and Pannonia. Despite this, one German bishop in particular, Wiching, continued his opposition, even forging pontifical documents in his own cause. Prevented, perhaps, from preaching and teaching as much as he would have wished, Methodius continued work on the translation of the Bible he had begun with his brother. After the death of Methodius in 884, Wiching drove his followers out of Moravia, undoing much of his work there.

78

# Methodius (14 June)

Methodius, who became patriarch of Constantinople, is revered for his courage and steadfastness during one of the periods of iconoclasm in the Eastern Churches, when icons or holy images were being destroyed and those who resisted this destruction were persecuted. He was born in Sicily and went first to Constantinople with the intention of serving at the imperial court, but was so impressed by a monk he met there that he decided to follow the religious life. He built a monastery on the island of Chios, intending to live out his days there, but was recalled to Constantinople by the patriarch Nicephorus, who was opposed to the destruction of icons under the emperor Leo the Armenian. Nicephorus was deposed and exiled and Methodius went to Rome. He returned to Constantinople in 821 under the new emperor, Michael II, bearing a letter from the pope asking for the reinstatement of Nicephorus, but the emperor instead ordered him to be scourged. For seven years he was confined in an underground prison with two thieves, one of whom, it is said, died and was left to rot. Persecution continued under Michael's successor, Theophilus, but when he died in 842 his widow, Theodora, acting as regent for her young son, ordered the restoration of icons, to general rejoicing. Methodius became patriarch the following year, Nicephorus having died in 828. During the remaining four years of his life he established an annual festival, known as the feast of Orthodoxy, to mark the victory over iconoclasm.

# Luke the Younger (7 February)

Luke, known to the Greeks as 'the Wonderworker', was born into a family of simple farmers in Thessaly at some time in the late 9th century. As a child he was known for his piety and charity; he would strip off his clothes and give them to beggars, and when he was sent out to sow he would scatter half the seed on the fields of the poor - legend has it that both their crops and his father's gave abundant yields.

While still a boy he felt a call to the religious life, but this was resisted by his family. On one occasion, after the death of his father, he left home to become a monk, but was captured and for a time imprisoned by soldiers who took him for a runaway slave. At length, two monks who were being given hospitality by his mother on their way to the Holy Land persuaded her to let the boy travel with them as far as Athens. There he joined a monastery, but before long was sent home again.

After four months, his mother at last relented. He left home for the last time at the age of seventeen and built himself a hermitage on Mount Ioannitsa near Corinth, where he lived for the remainder of his days. He became known as a miraculous healer, and was on one occasion witnessed elevated from the ground in prayer. He died c.946.

# Matilda (14 March)

Matilda was the wife of the tenth century German king Henry the Fowler and mother of, among others, Otto I, who became Holy Roman Emperor. After her husband's death she suffered ill-treatment from Otto for favouring his younger brother, Henry, who challenged him for the crown. Even after she had reconciled the two of them, both Otto and Henry complained that she gave away too much of the family's wealth to the poor and to the Church. During her life she founded several monasteries and convents, in one of which, Nordhausen, she spent her last days. She died in 968, aged about seventy-five, with a great reputation among the people for her kindness and goodness.

# Wenceslas of Bohemia  (28 September)

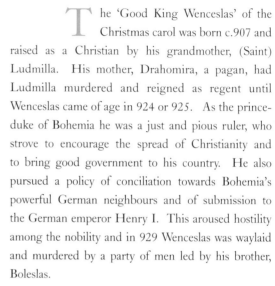

The 'Good King Wenceslas' of the Christmas carol was born c.907 and raised as a Christian by his grandmother, (Saint) Ludmilla. His mother, Drahomira, a pagan, had Ludmilla murdered and reigned as regent until Wenceslas came of age in 924 or 925. As the prince-duke of Bohemia he was a just and pious ruler, who strove to encourage the spread of Christianity and to bring good government to his country. He also pursued a policy of conciliation towards Bohemia's powerful German neighbours and of submission to the German emperor Henry I. This aroused hostility among the nobility and in 929 Wenceslas was waylaid and murdered by a party of men led by his brother, Boleslas.

Although their deaths were brought about mainly for political reasons he and his grandmother were almost immediately regarded as saints and martyrs, and Wenceslas remains to this day the patron saint of the Czechs.

*Detail from St Wenceslas, Czech School (16th century)*

# Dunstan (19 May)

Dunstan was born c.909 near Glastonbury. He belonged to a noble Anglo-Saxon family related to the ruling house of Wessex, was taken as a boy into the court of King Athelstan, and might have remained a courtier had not his recovery from a serious illness in his youth determined him to follow the religious life. For a time he lived at Glastonbury as a solitary monk, dividing his time between prayer, study and work; he had great skill as a metal-worker and as a copyist and illuminator of manuscripts and was also a gifted singer and harpist.

Then, about 943, King Edmund appointed him abbot of Glastonbury and called on him to revive English monasticism, which had virtually ceased to exist during the Viking invasions. With the help of other bishops, notably Ethelwold of Winchester and Oswald of York, he restored most of the great monasteries and founded new ones, and he was no less active in reforming the morals of the clergy and in establishing throughout the country an English version of the rule of St Benedict. Dunstan himself became archbishop of Canterbury in 959.

During the reign of King Edwy, 955-59, Dunstan was driven into exile in Flanders after criticizing the young king's conduct, but he served all the other kings who succeeded Athelstan as their principal advisor, in effect an ecclesiastical 'prime minister'. The rite he compiled for the coronation of Edgar as king of England in 973 is the basis of the coronation rite in use for the British sovereign today.

Dunstan died peacefully at Canterbury in 988.

*St Dunstan writing (British Library MS)*

# Stephen of Hungary

(16 August)

The first king of Hungary was born c.975, the son of the Magyar duke Geza. At about the age of ten he was baptized along with his father, who had seen the political expediency of becoming at least nominally Christian. Previously called Vaik, he was given the Christian name Istvan, or Stephen. He succeeded to his father's dukedom in 997 and, having established his rule over the whole country, was given a royal crown by Pope Sylvester II and became Hungary's first king in 1001. He then set about the conversion of his people, establishing bishoprics and monasteries, and suppressing pagan practices with all the ruthlessness of his age.

His last years were embittered by quarrels over the succession to his crown, following the death of his son and heir, Emeric, in a hunting accident in 1031. He died at Buda in 1038, his place in history secured as the man who turned the wild and disputatious Magyar tribesmen into the unified and law-abiding realm of Hungary.

*King Stephen by Pierre Joseph Verhaghen (1728-1811)*

# Olaf of Norway (29 July)

Olaf was born in 995, the son of a Norwegian nobleman. As a boy he became a viking and fought for Richard of Normandy and for the English king Ethelred II against the Danes. In 1016 he made himself king of Norway. Having recently been baptized, he brought Christian clergy into the country from abroad and used considerable ruthlessness in trying to extirpate paganism and impose the new religion on his people. His rule in consequence became deeply unpopular and it was not long before he was driven out by the Anglo-Danish king Canute. He was killed in 1030 at a battle on the Trondheim fjord while trying to regain his kingdom with the help of Swedish troops.

Despite his unpopularity during his life, his death was regarded as a martyrdom and he became Norway's hero-saint, and a symbol of national independence. His shrine at Nidaros (Trondheim) became a place of pilgrimage.

# Peter Damian (21 February)

Peter was born in Ravenna in 1001. Orphaned in infancy, he was left in the care of an older brother, who treated him virtually as a slave. Another brother, Damian, having found him employed as a swineherd, rescued him from this life and saw to it that he was given a thorough education in the schools of Lombardy; in gratitude to this brother, who was a priest, he adopted the name Peter Damian.

He himself became a teacher, but had already taken to a life of fasting, prayer and charitable works before, at the age of 34, he joined a hermitage which followed a strict version of the Benedictine rule. There he devoted himself to study of the scriptures, but his fellow monks unanimously elected him to take over the government of the community on the abbot's death. He accepted, very reluctantly, and in due course founded five other hermitages under his own direction. Such was his reputation for learning and for piety that he was called upon by successive popes to serve the Church on diplomatic missions outside his community. In 1057 he was prevailed upon to leave it altogether in order to become cardinal-bishop of Ostia, effectively the ruler of that city, but as soon as he was permitted to do so he returned to a life of solitary study and prayer.

He died in 1072. As a reformer of the Church he has a reputation for puritan severity, but throughout his life he practised the austerity that he recommended to others.

# Edward the Confessor

E dward was born in 1003, the son of Ethelred the Unready and Emma, sister of Duke Richard II of Normandy. In the period of Danish supremacy in England he was sent to Normandy for safety and during the years he spent there he developed Norman sympathies which were to remain with him when he succeeded to the English throne in 1042. In 1045 he married Edith, daughter of the powerful Earl Godwin of Wessex, but was never completely successful in establishing his authority against the Saxon nobility, of whom Godwin was the effective leader. He died in 1066 and was succeeded by Harold, Earl Godwin's son. Norman claims that he had promised the succession to William of Normandy led to William's invasion and his defeat of Harold at Hastings. Edward's name 'the Confessor' derives from the fact that he confessed, or bore witness to, Christ through his life's example. Throughout his reign he was devout, credited with miracles – he was the first sovereign to bestow 'the king's touch' against scrofula – peace-loving, and generous to the poor. He and his wife were childless, reputedly because they were celibate. He founded the abbey church of Westminster and his remains were kept there in their shrine after it was pulled down and rebuilt in the thirteenth century.

Edward was canonized in 1161.

*Edward the Confessor by Jean de Boulogne Giambologna (1529-1608)*

# Bruno (6 October)

The founder of the Carthusian Order was born into a noble family in Cologne c.1033. He was educated at the cathedral school of Rheims and, after becoming a priest, taught theology there for twenty years. In 1076, having become chancellor, he denounced his archbishop, Manasses, as worldly and corrupt and for having obtained his see by purchase. For this Bruno was discharged from his office. After Manasses had been excommunicated and deposed Bruno returned for a time to Rheims, but in 1084, with six companions, he withdrew to a wild and mountainous piece of land near Grenoble known as La Grande Chartreuse. There they founded the first monastery of the kind known to this day as a chartreuse (in English a 'charterhouse'), in which the monks live in solitude in their cells and come together only for worship. The rule of the Carthusian Order was (and still is) a strict one, of worship, physical labour, study and penitence, but it attracted many recruits.

In 1090 Bruno was summoned to Rome to serve Pope Urban II, a former pupil of his, as advisor. He went reluctantly, never to see his brothers at La Grande Chartreuse again. Before long the pope released him, but would not let him return to France. Instead he founded two other charterhouses near Squillace in Calabria, and it was at one of them that he died in 1101.

*St Bruno by Pier Francesco Mola (1612-66)*

# Anselm (21 April)

Anselm, one of the greatest of medieval theologians and philosophers, was born at Aosta in Piedmont c.1033, the son of a Lombard nobleman. His father resisted his early desire to become a monk, and it was not until 1059 that he entered the monastery of Bec in Normandy, where he became the pupil, and later the friend, of its prior, Lanfranc. When Lanfranc became abbot of Caen, Anselm succeeded him as prior of Bec. He was elected abbot in 1078. In his years at Bec he wrote many of his most important works: on the proofs of the existence of God, on the nature of truth and the question of free will, on the origin of evil, on the art of reasoning.

Meanwhile, Lanfranc had become archbishop of Canterbury. Three years after his death, in 1093, Anselm was accepted by King William Rufus as his successor. His public life thereafter was largely determined by disputes with England's kings, first William, then Henry I, over the great medieval question of relations between church and state, and in particular over the crown's right to interfere in the appointment of bishops and abbots. Standing up firmly for the Church's position, Anselm was twice obliged to spend two periods of exile abroad. During the first of these, in Rome, he wrote his most famous work, *Cur Deus Homo?*, on the question of why God had been obliged to become man in order to atone for the sins of mankind. While in England he encouraged the ordination of native Englishmen, enforced celibacy among his clergy, and actively opposed slavery.

Records of the time speak of the great charm of his nature, which made him greatly loved by men of all classes. He died at Canterbury in 1109 and was canonized and declared a doctor of the Church in 1720.

# Margaret of Scotland (16 November)

Queen Margaret of Scotland was born c.1045, probably in Hungary, the daughter of Edward, the exiled son of Edmund Ironside, king of the English. She and her German mother returned to England in 1057, but after the Norman conquest they were obliged to take refuge in Scotland, where in 1070 she married King Malcolm Canmore.

Deeply religious, she had a powerful influence on her rough and barely educated husband, softening his temper and polishing his manners and making of him a thoroughly Christian monarch. She also did much to civilize his court and his kingdom, promoting education and helping the poor. With Malcolm she founded many churches, most notably Dunfermline abbey. In private she lived a life of great austerity, fasting often and spending many hours in prayer.

Malcolm was treacherously killed at Alnwick in November 1093. Margaret died four days later and was buried at Dunfermline. Of their six sons, three – Edgar, Alexander and David – ruled Scotland in succession, while their daughter Matilda (or Maud) married Henry I of England.

Margaret was canonized in 1250 and named patroness of Scotland in 1673.

# Bernard of Clairvaux (20 August)

Bernard was born in 1090 at a castle near Dijon in Burgundy, one of the six sons of a Burgundian nobleman. In 1113 he joined the new and strict monastery of Citeaux, along with four of his brothers and twenty-seven friends. Only two years later he was sent to found a daughter house at Clairvaux in Champagne. Under his direction this new monastery flourished and in turn created no fewer than sixty-eight daughter houses as far afield as Rievaulx in England and Mellifont in Ireland. Thus although he was not one of the founders of Citeaux he can fairly be claimed to be the founder of the great Cistercian Order that grew out of it, devoted to the restoration of simplicity and purity in monastic life.

Bernard was a great teacher, known in his time as *Doctor mellifluus*, 'the honey-sweet-tongued teacher'. But he was also actively engaged in the public affairs of his day, preaching against the Albigensians of Languedoc, urging kings and princes to undertake the Second Crusade (and being blamed for its failure), arbitrating in a disputed papal election, attacking the teachings of Peter Abelard and denouncing the persecution of the Jews in the Rhineland. He died at Clairvaux in 1153 and was canonized in 1174.

*St Bernard, Abbot of Clairvaux by Jean Fouquet (c.1420-80)*

# Hildegard of Bingen (17 September)

The great medieval mystic and composer was born at Bermersheim in 1098. Although she was to live to be eighty she endured ill health from childhood. As a child, too, she had the first of the visionary experiences which were to continue throughout her life, and which she described in her writings. She took the veil at the age of fifteen and in 1136 became prioress of the neighbouring Benedictine convent. In 1147 she moved her community to Rupertsberg, near Bingen, on the Rhine, where she built a great convent. From there, now famous, she reported her mysterious visions, some of them prophetic, and corresponded at length with four popes, two emperors, King Henry II of England, and many other prominent laymen and clergy, including Bernard of Clairvaux.

Aside from her visionary writings, of which the principal one is called *Scivias*, Hildegard also wrote books on science and medicine, commentaries on the Gospels and on the Benedictine rule, poems and hymns. She also composed a great deal of music, whose highly individual quality has only recently come to be recognized in modern times. She wrote of music that it was 'a symbol of the harmony which Satan has broken, which helps man to build a bridge of holiness between this world and the World of all Beauty and Music'.

*The Vision of St Hildegard by Battista Dossi (c.1474-1548)*

# Thomas of Canterbury

(29 December)

Thomas Becket was born into a wealthy Norman family in London in 1118. After a sound education, he rose rapidly through the ranks of the Church while also being closely involved in public affairs. In 1154 he was appointed archdeacon of Canterbury; in 1155 King Henry II made him his chancellor. Becket served the king faithfully for seven years as a statesman and diplomat but also as his friend and companion in the pursuit of aristocratic pleasure, leading the life of a brilliant and worldly courtier-cleric. In 1162, however, when the see of Canterbury fell vacant, he became archbishop. At once a great change came over him; he adopted an austere style of life and took his pastoral duties seriously, keeping to a strict rule of daily prayer, study and attendance at mass and being particularly generous in alms-giving and rigorous in the selection of candidates for holy orders.

Becket, however, had always been a man of intense and obdurate pride, with a violent temper, and he remained so when he began to come into conflict with his friend the king. As archbishop of Canterbury he was second only to the king in England, and like most churchmen of his day he would have claimed that in certain matters he outranked him. His eventual downfall and martyrdom epitomized the great dispute between church and state that dominated Europe in the middle ages. The chief, though not the only, issue in Becket's case was the question of which should have jurisdiction over clergy convicted of crimes. The conflict became increasingly bitter, and in 1164, following a stormy council at Northampton, during which he was threatened with prosecution, he fled to France.

In 1170, following years of negotiation involving the pope and the king of France, Becket returned to England, apparently reconciled, but the quarrel immediately flared up again. Henry, himself in Normandy at the time, angrily pronounced the words, 'Who will rid me of this turbulent priest?' Four knights took him at his word and set off for England, their names being Reginald Fitzurse, William de Tracy, Hugh de Morville and Richard le Breton. On 29 December they came upon Becket in his cathedral and after loud altercations struck him dead with their swords.

News of the murder spread rapidly throughout Christendom. Thomas Becket was spontaneously acclaimed as a martyr and formally canonized in 1173. Henry, who had almost certainly not intended his death, had to do public penance of the most humiliating kind, his reputation as one of the greatest of medieval kings permanently tarnished.

*Murder of Thomas Becket, from a book of Psalms (13th century)*          *St Thomas Becket by Girolamo da Santacroce (1556-?)*

# William of Norwich (24 March)

I n 1144 the mutilated body of a twelve-year-old boy was found in a wood outside Norwich. His murderer was never found, but five years later it began to be alleged that he was a victim of the Jews, who had killed him for ritual purposes. William was venerated locally as a martyr. This is the earliest recorded instance of an accusation against the Jews that became all too common in the later middle ages. No case has ever been substantiated, but what has been called 'one of the most notable and disastrous lies in history' helped to feed a rampant anti-Semitism.

# Dominic (8 August)

T he founder of the preaching order known as the Dominicans was born at Calaruega in Castile in 1170. He became a cathedral canon at the age of twenty-six and in 1206 accompanied his bishop, Diego, on a mission to the heretical Cathars or Albigensians in Languedoc. Both men attempted to bring the Albigensians back to orthodoxy by gentle reasoning, and Dominic and his handful of followers continued to do so after the death of Diego at the end of 1207. This coincided with the murder by the Albigensians of the papal legate, Peter de Castelnau, and the start of a brutal campaign, led by Simon de Montfort, to destroy the heresy by force. Dominic, a man of deep compassion, would have had to watch as cities and towns were destroyed and their inhabitants indiscriminately slaughtered.

In 1215, in Toulouse, Dominic began to form the order that bears his name: a body of rigorously trained priests, living monastically, but devoted to preaching and teaching anywhere in the world. The Dominicans would play a major role in the intellectual and spiritual life of Christendom in the later middle ages. Dominic himself spent the remaining years of his life travelling, preaching and establishing new friaries. He died at Bologna in 1221 and was canonized in 1234.

*Bust of St Dominic, Catalan School (c.1450)*

# Francis of Assisi (4 October)

The founder of the preaching order that bears his name was born in Assisi in Umbria c.1181, the son of a merchant. For some years he led the frivolous life of a wealthy young man, but, in his early twenties, following some months as a prisoner-of-war during fighting between Assisi and Perugia and a long period of illness, he began to feel strong religious impulses which led him to care for the sick and the poor. One day, when he was about twenty-five, he was praying in a church just outside Assisi when he seemed to hear the image of Christ saying to him, 'Francis, go and repair my falling house'. Taking these words literally, he removed some goods from his father's warehouse and sold them to provide money for repairing the church. For this deed his father disinherited him, and he took this as a sign that he was to give up all possessions and 'wed Lady Poverty'.

Others began to follow him as he went around Italy preaching and calling the people to repentance, and in 1210 Pope Innocent III recognized Francis and his eleven companions as Friars Minor, 'lesser brothers'. In 1212, with (Saint) Clare of Assisi, Francis founded the first community of Poor Ladies, known in England as the Poor Clares. In 1219 he accompanied crusaders to Egypt and visited the Holy Land.

The Franciscans lived lives of extreme simplicity, renouncing not only property of any kind but also learning and any kind of rank, relying entirely on alms for their sustenance. By 1220 they had become a religious order, their numbers had greatly grown and they were being sent abroad as far as England.

*St Francis of Assisi by Giotto di Bondone (c.1266-1337)*

In 1224 Francis himself, while fasting, had a vision of the crucifixion so intense that it left on his hands, feet and body the marks of the five wounds of Christ. These stigmata remained with him until his death two years later. He has been revered ever since for his humility and spirituality and for his intense love of God's creation, expressed in his speaking of 'brother sun' and 'sister moon' and of his own body as 'brother donkey'. Since 1979 he has been the patron saint of ecologists.

# Antony of Padua (13 June)

The great medieval preacher and doctor of the Church was born in Lisbon in 1195 and worked in Portugal as a canon regular until, at the age of twenty-five, he joined a Franciscan mission to the Muslims of Morocco. Ill health, however, obliged him to leave almost immediately and return to Europe. For a time he lived as a hermit near Forlí in Italy. It was there, however, that he revealed his gift as a preacher, with a powerful voice, remarkable eloquence and an extraordinarily profound knowledge of scripture. He was sent to preach all over northern Italy, bringing many sinners and heretics back to righteousness. He is described as a small, slightly corpulent man, but with an attractive, radiant personality. From 1226 he made his home in Padua. He died in 1231, aged only thirty-six, and was canonized the following year. In 1232 work began on the great church at Padua that holds his tomb and bears his name.

# Albert the Great (Albertus Magnus)

## (15 November)

Albert was born into a noble family in Swabia in 1206. He studied at the university of Padua, where he joined the recently formed Dominican order but absorbed himself in the study of Aristotle. From 1248 he taught at Cologne, where his pupils included Thomas Aquinas, who became a lifelong friend. In 1260 he became bishop of Regensburg, but he resigned after two years, preferring to devote himself to study and teaching.

Albert is known as 'the universal teacher' for his encyclopedic learning. As a doctor of the Church his fame rests on his application of Aristotelian principles and methods to the study of theology, but his voluminous writings include work on logic, metaphysics, ethics, physics, geography, astronomy, mineralogy, chemistry, biology, botany and physiology. The range of his learning so astonished his contemporaries that a legend grew up that he had magical powers.

He was canonized and named a doctor of the Church in 1931. At the same time he was named patron saint of all students of the natural sciences.

# Louis of France

(25 August)

Louis IX was born at Poissy in 1214, became king of France, on the death of his father, at the age of twelve, and took over the rule of his kingdom from the regency of his mother, Blanche of Castile, in 1235. From the first he was the ideal of a medieval Christian monarch. He was devout, pure and charitable in his private life, detesting profanity and forbidding it to be used in his presence. In the testament he left to his son, he advised, 'Make sure that you never willingly do or say anything which, should it come to light, you could not gladly admit to'. In public he defended the poor against the powerful, including his own nobles. He was also an able administrator, under whom France prospered, and a successful soldier, defeating the English king Henry III at Taillebourg in 1242. It was Louis who built the stupendous Gothic edifice, the Sainte Chapelle, in Paris, to house an important relic, the crown of thorns, awarded to him by Baldwin II, the Latin emperor in Constantinople.

As a crusader, for which he is most famous, he was less successful. The crusade he led in 1248 had early successes but was heavily defeated in 1250 and Louis himself was taken prisoner and had to be ransomed. On a later venture, in 1270, he died of dysentery soon after landing at Tunis. He was canonized in 1297.

Detail from: *St Louis of France, Flemish School (15th century)*

# Thomas Aquinas (28 January)

Thomas Aquinas, possibly the greatest of the medieval doctors of the Church, was born c.1225, the son of a nobleman of Lombard descent, and educated among the Benedictines at Monte Cassino and at the university of Naples. When, in his twentieth year, he decided to join the Dominican order, his family were so outraged that his brothers seized him and locked him up for a year. Thomas, however, would not be dissuaded. On his release he went to study in Paris and Cologne. He became a master of theology in 1256 and spent the rest of his life studying, teaching and writing. He left Paris in 1259 to teach in several Italian cities; from 1269-1272 he was in Paris again; the last two years of his life were spent in Naples. He died in 1274 on a journey to a general council at Lyons, summoned to attempt a reconciliation of the Roman and Greek Orthodox churches.

Of his many written works, the most famous and influential is his *Summa Theologica*, still the classic exposition of Christian theology. Vast though it is, he left it unfinished after receiving a revelation during mass in December 1273, declaring, 'All I have written seems to me like so much straw compared with what I have seen and what has been revealed to me'.

*St Thomas Aquinas by Sandro Botticelli (1444/5-1510)*

# Catherine of Siena (29 April)

Catherine was born in 1347 in Siena, where her father was a prosperous dyer. As a child of six she had the first of many mystical experiences and felt a strong vocation to the religious life. At twelve, her parents began to urge her to prepare herself for marriage, but she patiently resisted their increasingly cruel treatment of her and at last, when she was about twenty, was allowed to enter the Dominican order as a tertiary sister. This meant that she wore the habit but continued to live at home.

Her ecstatic experiences continued; she had visions of Jesus, and in 1375 suffered the pain of the stigmata, the marks of which, it was claimed, were visible after her death. From the first, however, she had felt called to work in the world for the salvation of her neighbours, caring for the sick and healing disputes. She soon attracted a group of followers from all classes in Siena whom she called her 'family'. Her reputation for holiness spread. She was called upon to act as a mediator in the quarrels between the Italian cities and the papacy, and in this connection she travelled to Pisa and to Avignon, where the papacy then resided. She also persuaded Pope Gregory XI to return from Avignon to Rome, but after his death, when a rival pope emerged in Avignon and the 'great schism' that divided Western Christendom began, her support for his successor, Urban VI, had less success. She wrote letters on his behalf to the leading princes and churchmen of Europe, but could not overcome the unpopularity that Urban's own character brought on him. She was in Rome, still busily engaged in this crisis, when she fell ill and died in 1380. She was canonized in 1461.

Previous page: *St Catherine of Siena by Gerolamo di Benvenuto (1470-1542)*

*The Mystic Marriage of St Catherine of Siena by Fra Bartolomeo (1475-1517)*

# Joan of Arc (30 May)

Jeanne la Pucelle, or Joan the Maid, was fourteen when she emerged from her obscurity in the year 1428, at a time when a large part of France was occupied by the English, in alliance with the Burgundians. The French ruler, Charles, the Dauphin, had succeeded his father, Charles VI in 1422, but Rheims, where he should have been crowned, was in English hands, and he seemed to have despaired of the struggle to free his country from its enemies.

Joan was born at Domrémy in Champagne. Her parents were peasants, and she was illiterate, but her mother was a devout and loving parent and the child grew up to be notably pious. From about her thirteenth year she began to hear what she called her 'voices', calling her to save France and to lead the Dauphin to his coronation at Rheims. At their urging she went to the nearby town of Vaucouleurs and asked the French commander there, de Baudricourt, to help her, but he dismissed her with mockery. She returned to Domrémy, but the voices continued to press her.

She returned to de Baudricourt, who, this time, was more inclined to heed her, having received news of a serious defeat near Orléans which Joan had predicted. On 6 March 1429 she was received by the Dauphin at Chinon. Although he was impressed by various signs she gave him, his courtiers were naturally highly sceptical. For three weeks she was examined by a body of churchmen at Poitiers, who at length advised Charles that she was neither mad nor an impostor. She was given a suit of armour and put at the head of a French army which by the beginning of May had defeated the English besieging Orléans.

After further victories she persuaded Charles to march on Rheims. He was crowned there on 17 July 1429, with Joan at his side, her mission now accomplished. The king and the French nobility, however, showed little eagerness to follow up the success she had brought them. After a failed attempt to regain Paris, at which she was wounded, and a period of truce, she went off to relieve the besieged city of Compiègne. There she was captured by the Burgundians, who held her prisoner for several months before selling her to the English. King Charles during that time made no attempt to save her.

In February 1431 she went on trial, charged with sorcery and heresy. She replied to the questions with courage, quiet dignity, intelligence and even wit, but the verdict was inevitable; unless she retracted she must be handed over to the secular arm and executed. Faced with a terrible death, she wavered briefly but then firmly re-asserted that she had obeyed messages sent to her by God, and even resumed male dress, the wearing of which had been part of the indictment against her. She went to the stake at Rouen on 30 May 1431, being then barely twenty years old.

In 1456 a commission set up by Pope Callixtus III at the request of her family declared her conviction to be fraudulent and fully rehabilitated her. She was canonized in 1920, not for her military services to her country but for the virtue of her personal life and the resoluteness of her faith.

*Joan of Arc by Dante Gabriel Rossetti (1828-82)*

# Thomas More (22 June)

Thomas More, the English humanist and martyr, was born in London in 1478, the son of a judge. He studied at Oxford and Lincoln's Inn and was admitted to the bar in 1501. In 1504 he entered Parliament. He was a young man of great brilliance, learning and wit, who met and corresponded with many of the humanist thinkers of the day, among them his friends John Fisher (who was also martyred and who shares his feast-day), John Colet, Thomas Linacre and Desiderius Erasmus. In the great religious debate of the day he sided with those moderates who, though strongly opposed to Martin Luther, argued for reason and toleration. He married Jane Colt in 1505 and with her had three daughters and a son, all of whom he took care to educate thoroughly. His beloved wife Jane died in 1510 but within a year he had re-married, to Alice Middleton, a widow, so as to have a mother for his young children.

In 1516 he completed his most famous work, *Utopia*, a description of an ideal but attainable society elevated above narrow self-interest. Meanwhile he was rising rapidly in the law and in the service of King Henry VIII, whose friend he had become. In 1529 he was appointed Lord Chancellor in succession to the disgraced Thomas Wolsey. As such he was the most powerful man in the realm after the king himself, but the post was a poisoned chalice. Henry, wishing to re-marry, demanded that his marriage with Katherine of Aragon be nullified so that he could marry Anne Boleyn. More, believing the marriage to be valid, refused to agree. The king declared himself supreme head of the Church in England and began to take measures against the authority of Rome. In 1532 More resigned his office and for fifteen months he lived quietly, although in near-poverty. Then in 1534 he and his friend Bishop Fisher refused to take an oath recognizing the succession of the children of Anne Boleyn, declaring the king's marriage to Katherine invalid and repudiating the authority of the Pope. For this refusal More was imprisoned in the Tower. During that time he wrote his *Dialogue of Comfort against Tribulation*, the finest of his spiritual works. In June 1535 John Fisher was executed. Nine days later More was put on trial for treason in Westminster Hall, found guilty, and sentenced to death. He said to his judges that he wished 'we may yet hereafter in Heaven merrily all meet together to everlasting salvation'. Before his execution by beheading on Tower Hill, he told the crowd of spectators that he was 'the king's good servant – but God's first'.

Thomas More was canonized, along with John Fisher, in 1935. He is the patron saint of lawyers.

*Sir Thomas More by Hans Holbein the Younger (1497/8-1543)*

# Ignatius of Loyola (31 July)

The founder of the Society of Jesus, or Jesuits, was born at Loyola, probably in 1491, the son of a Basque nobleman of ancient family; his baptismal name was Inigo. As a young man he fought as a soldier, and it was while recovering from a serious leg wound received at the siege of Pamplona in 1521 that he began to read religious books, particularly lives of the saints, and at length resolved to devote his life to God. After a year of meditation and prayer at Manresa in Catalonia he went on pilgrimage to Rome and Jerusalem and then spent ten years in intensive study, eventually graduating as master of arts from the university of Paris.

While in Paris, Ignatius became the leading figure of a small group of pious laymen who in 1534 took a vow to be missionaries to the Moslems in the Holy Land. Three years later, now ten in number, they met in Venice but, finding the way to Palestine blocked by war, decided instead to go to Rome and offer their services to Pope Paul III. All were ordained to the priesthood, and soon afterwards formed themselves into a religious order which, as well as the usual vows of poverty, chastity and obedience, took a further one to be at the pope's disposal at any time and wherever they might be. They already called themselves 'the company of Jesus' and in 1540 Pope Paul III formally recognized them as the Company (or Society) of Jesus.

From the first the order devoted itself to mission work and in 1547 it began the important services to education that it continues in Catholic countries to this day. Its numbers grew from ten to one thousand. Ignatius himself remained in Rome, directing its activities around the world as its first superior general, until his death in 1556. The Society of Jesus was at the forefront of resistance to the Protestant Reformation, but in this matter Ignatius stressed the importance of offering an example of charity and moderation and of showing courtesy to opponents while pointing out their errors.

During his retirement at Manresa he began work on his most famous book, the *Spiritual Exercises*, which was finally published in 1548 and is still hugely influential throughout the Christian world today. Ignatius was canonized in 1622.

*Saint Ignatius of Loyola, French School (17th century)*

# John of God (8 March)

This John was born in Portugal in 1495 and served as a soldier in the Franco-Spanish wars and against the Turks before, at the age of forty, he was assailed by a conviction that his life hitherto had been wasted in sin and must be redeemed. He began a business of selling sacred tracts and pictures, at first in Gibraltar, then in Granada. In that city, in 1538, he heard a sermon by the famous preacher John of Avila which so affected him that he gave away his entire stock and took to roaming about the streets, screaming and tearing his hair, and behaving in such a demented fashion that he was confined in a lunatic asylum. John of Avila came to visit him there and at last persuaded him that he could redeem his sins better by serving others than by solitary penance.

John left the asylum, started selling wood in the market-place to earn money, and then, with the help of the archbishop of Granada, took a house in which to look after the sick and destitute, not excluding lepers, beggars, prostitutes and the insane. All these he cared for with such devotion and practical wisdom that his work won the financial support of pious wealthy women of the city and others came to assist him in the service of the poor.

He died in 1550, probably from a fever contracted while trying to rescue a drowning man in a flood. Six years after his death, his followers founded an order of hospitallers, the Brothers of St John of God, whose work spread throughout Catholic Europe.

# Francis Xavier

(3 December)

The great Jesuit missionary was born near Pamplona in Spanish Navarre in 1506. He was one of the seven students who came together in Paris in 1534 to form the group that would become the Society of Jesus. In 1541 Ignatius Loyola sent him to be a missionary in India. After a journey lasting over a year he arrived in Goa, then under Portuguese rule. He spent seven years working in southern India, Ceylon and the Malay peninsula. During that time he was greatly distressed by the depravity of many of the Europeans there and by their brutal exploitation of the native peoples, about which he wrote with great frankness to the king of Portugal. He made many conversions, though mainly among the lower castes; he had little success with educated Indians, whose own religious beliefs he did not attempt to understand.

In 1549 he sailed for Japan, where he was well received by the authorities and given permission to teach. Having learned some Japanese, he made several thousand converts, though fewer than he had hoped. After two years he returned to Goa and then, in 1552, set out for China, at that time closed to all foreigners. He landed on the island of Shangchwan, near the mouth of the Canton river, but while waiting for a junk whose master had agreed to bring him secretly ashore on the mainland he fell ill. He died two weeks later, aged forty-six, alone except for one young Chinese Christian.

Francis Xavier was canonized in 1622 and is the patron saint of Roman Catholic missionaries.

*St Francis Xavier by Nicolas Poussin (1594-1665)*

# Teresa of Avila (15 October)

Teresa was born at Avila in Castile in 1515 and entered a Carmelite convent there in c.1535. After some years she began to have visions and ecstatic experiences, including the mystical piercing of her heart as if by a spear of divine love. She described these experiences extensively in her writings, without appearing to attach supreme importance to them.

The convent at Avila was a large, easy-going community which maintained many contacts with the outside world. In 1562 Teresa founded her own convent of St Joseph's, governed in accordance with the strict Carmelite rule, whose followers were 'discalced' or shoeless, i.e. barefoot. In the twenty years that followed she travelled around Spain founding seventeen further convents, all of them small, enclosed, strict, poor and devoted to prayer as their primary function.

Despite her visions, and the severity of her rule, Teresa was a cheerful, practical, warm and affectionate woman, with a personality that was attractive as well as authoritative. Her many surviving works include *The Way of Perfection*, written for the guidance of her own nuns, an account of her own life up to 1562, *The Book of Foundations*, an account of the establishment of her convents, and *The Interior Castle*, a work of spiritual enlightenment. It is mainly on account of the last of these that she was declared to be a doctor of the Church in 1970.

She died in 1582 and was canonized in 1622.

*St Teresa of Avila by Juan de la Miseria (c.1526-1616)*

# Philip Neri (26 May)

P hilip Neri, who became known as 'the Apostle of Rome', was born in Florence in 1515, the son of a prosperous notary. As a youth he was apprenticed to a relative for a career in business, but in his late teens he had a mystical experience which he later referred to as a 'conversion' and which led him to a conviction that he must renounce worldly pursuits and devote his life to God.

Around 1534 he went to Rome, at that time in a state of demoralization and religious decline following its sacking in 1527. For the first few years of his time there he devoted himself to prayer and the study of theology and philosophy. Then he began to work among the young men of the city, talking with them and encouraging them to help him care for the sick. He founded a confraternity of laymen who met for prayer and spiritual exercises and worked in the hospitals and for the care of poor pilgrims; in time this confraternity became the great hospital of the Holy Trinity.

In 1551 he was ordained a priest and went to live at the church of San Girolamo. Many, including the notables of the city, came to him for confession and to seek counsel; he was said to have the gift of reading hearts. With the help of other priests, he continued to hold conferences for worship and spiritual instruction. As the numbers attending these greatly increased a large room was built for them above the nave of the church. From the priests' practice of using a bell to call others to prayer in their oratory the group acquired the name the Oratorians. Properly speaking, however, this congregation was formed in 1564, when Philip installed a group of young priests to share a common table at the church of San Giovanni, of which he was rector. They observed a simple rule of life but were forbidden to take vows or renounce any property they had. In 1575 the pope formally recognized the Congregation of the Oratory, whose numbers had greatly increased, and gave them the ancient church of Santa Maria in Valicella, which Philip totally rebuilt with help from the Vatican and the rich men of the city.

Philip Neri was sometimes criticised for his unconventional methods and his emphasis on the idea that the path to spiritual perfection was open to laymen as well as to priests and monks and nuns. Among the people of Rome, however, he was greatly loved for his humility, gentleness and cheerfulness. He died, in his new church, in 1595, and was canonized in 1622.

*St Philip Neri by Guiseppe Angeli (1712-98)*

# Katherine dei Ricci (13 February)

This saint was born in 1522 into a distinguished Florentine family and given the name Alexandrina.

She took the name Katherine when she entered a Dominican convent at Prato at the age of thirteen. While still a young nun, she became novice mistress, then sub-prioress; at the age of twenty-nine she was elected prioress in perpetuity.

She was renowned outside her convent for holiness and wisdom, but is particularly famous for the series of ecstatic experiences she is recorded to have had every week for twelve years, during which she seemed to re-enact the scenes of the passion of Christ. Rumours of these miraculous experiences attracted such large crowds of visitors, disrupting the regular life of the convent, that on becoming prioress she asked her nuns to pray for her to be released from them. In 1554 they came to an end.

Deeply concerned for reform of the Church, she corresponded with leading figures in the reform movement, including St Philip Neri, who reported that she appeared and talked to him in a vision at Rome while she was physically still in her convent. She died in 1590 and was canonized in 1747.

# Edmund Campion (1 December)

The English Catholic martyr was born in 1540, the son of a London bookseller. He became a student and then a fellow of St John's College, Oxford, and was seen as a young man of great promise. He had become an Anglican deacon, but was increasingly troubled at the thought of taking holy orders in a church about which he had grave doubts. In 1571 he went to Douai and was received into the Roman Catholic church.

For some years he taught at the Jesuit college in Prague, but in 1580 he returned secretly to England. There, although constantly pursued by government agents, he preached almost daily in Berkshire, Oxfordshire, Northamptonshire and Lancashire. In June 1581 he created a sensation by distributing in the university church of Oxford four hundred copies of an anti-Anglican pamphlet that he had written. Efforts to capture him were redoubled, and in July of that year he was betrayed while holding mass at a house at Lyford, Berkshire, and arrested along with two other priests. He was held in the Tower and tortured, but refused to recant his beliefs. On 14 November he was put on trial in Westminster Hall on the false charge of having come to England to raise a rebellion against the queen. Despite torture, he conducted a skilful defence both of himself and of the other men charged with him, but was found guilty and sentenced to death. He was executed at Tyburn on 1 December. On the scaffold he prayed publicly for the queen, wishing her a long and prosperous reign. He was beatified in 1886 and canonized in 1970.

# John of the Cross (14 December)

B. IOANES. A CRVCE EXTATICVS. AT QVESVBLIMIS DOCTOR MISTYCVS
Carmelitarum excalceatorum PRIMVS PARENS dicti eiusdem reformationis fundatione S.Teresiæ a Iesu.
Io ... us Claruit miraculis ante, et post obitum, Cuis corpus usque hodie in ... septeris honorifice ... tur

John de Yepes was born at Avila in 1542 and became a Carmelite friar at the age of twenty-one. Under the influence of Teresa of Avila he devoted himself to establishing the reformed or 'discalced' ('shoeless') order of Carmelites, taking the religious name John of the Cross. The reforms were violently opposed by some of the 'calced' or mitigated Carmelites and in 1577 John was imprisoned and severely beaten by order of the vicar general. It was while in prison that he began writing the great mystical poems for which he is now remembered. He escaped after nine months and resumed his work in the reformed order, while continuing to write, but after the death of Teresa disagreements arose among the discalced themselves. John took the side of the moderates in these disputes. When at length the more extreme party triumphed he was dismissed from his offices and sent to a remote friary. After some months there he fell ill and was sent to the convent of Ubeda, whose prior was one of his enemies. Here again he was treated with great cruelty until a few months before his death in December 1591.

John was canonized in 1726 and named a doctor of the Church in 1926 for his writings in mystical theology. His poems were translated into English by the South African poet Roy Campbell. The most famous, *The Dark Night of the Soul*, speaks of the journey from utter desolation through a personal experience of the crucifixion to a sense of mystical union with the glory of God.

*St John of the Cross, Spanish School (18th century)*

# Francis de Sales (24 January)

The great doctor of the Church was born in 1567 near Annecy in Savoy and educated there and at the universities of Paris and Padua. He became a priest in 1593 and was given as his first mission the task of bringing back to Roman Catholicism the people of his own part of France, who had turned to Calvinism; in this he had great success, thanks to his gift for preaching. In 1602 he became bishop of Geneva, the heartland of Calvinism. Residing at Annecy he became greatly beloved, particularly by children, for his great kindness, gentleness and humility. In 1604, while attending a course in Dijon, he met Jane de Chantal, herself later canonized, with whom, in 1610, he founded the Order of Visitation. It was at the Visitation convent at Lyons that he died in 1622.

In his role as spiritual advisor and in his devotional writings he stressed the possibility of living a holy life among the realities of this world, whether as soldier, shopkeeper, bureaucrat or courtier. His book, *Introduction to the Devout Life*, was admired by, among others, the Protestant King James I and John Wesley. A Calvinist minister of Geneva said of him, 'If we honoured any man as a saint, I know no one since the days of the apostles more worthy of it than this man'. He was canonized in 1655. Pope Pius XI declared him to be the patron saint of journalists.

*St Francis of Sales, Bishop of Geneva, by Giambattista Tiepolo (1696-1770)*

# Vincent de Paul (27 September)

The founder of the Congregation of the Mission and the Sisters of Charity was born in Gascony in c.1580, the son of a poor peasant, and became a priest at the early age of twenty. His ambition at first was to live a life of comfort, and as one of the chaplains of Queen Margaret of Valois he received the income of a small abbey. In Paris, however, he came under the influence of Pierre de Bérulle, later cardinal, and through him became confessor to the devout Countess de Gondi and tutor to her children. This influence, and his work among spiritually ignorant peasants and convicts, brought about a great change in him, and he dedicated himself thereafter to the spiritual and material welfare of the poor. He became chaplain to the French galley fleet (of which Mme de Gondi's husband was captain-general) and provided a mission to the convicts who manned the galleys at Bordeaux. In 1625, with the help of the de Gondis, he founded the Congregation of the Mission, a body of priests dedicated to missionary work among the poor, especially in the countryside, and to the training of clergy. In 1633 he founded the Sisters of Charity, devoted to the sick poor. With his connections among wealthy and pious women he was also able to found several hospitals, including one for galley-slaves at Marseilles, although the last was never completed.

During his lifetime his movement spread as far as Ireland in the west and Poland in the east; it is now worldwide. He died in 1660 and was canonized in 1737. The society of charitable laymen that bears his name was founded in Paris in 1833.

# Joseph Maria Tomassi (3 January)

Honoured by the Church for his profound learning and the sanctity of his life, Joseph Maria Tomassi was born in 1649 in Sicily, where his father was Duke of Palermo and Prince of Lampedusa. He came from a family devoted to monastic life; his four sisters all became nuns, his mother also entered a convent, and when he was fifteen and declared his intention to become a monk he discovered that his father wished to do the same, leaving his titles and estates to his son. The Duke relented, however, and Joseph Maria became a novice of the Theatine order in Palermo. There he devoted himself to the study of Greek and Hebrew and to textual scholarship, but was noted also for his great humility and for many acts of charity.

When offered the cardinalate by Pope Clement XI he at first declined it, finally accepting the honour only in May 1712, just a few months before his death. He was beatified in 1803 and canonized by John Paul II in 1986.

*St Vincent de Paul by Jean Andre (1662-1753)*

# Elizabeth Seton (4 January)

Elizabeth Bayley Seton, the first native-born American to be canonized, was born in New York in 1774. Her father was a noted physician and a professor of anatomy and her family were mostly devout Protestants. In 1794 she married a wealthy merchant, William Seton, by whom she had five children, but his business and his health failed, and he died in 1803 in Italy, where he had gone to seek a cure. His widow stayed on for some months in Italy where, already naturally pious, she was strongly drawn to Roman Catholicism. Two years later, having returned to the United States, she was received into the Church. This act estranged her from her family, but she was soon after invited to open a Catholic school for girls in Baltimore, which in time became the model for parochial schools across the United States.

Even before her conversion Elizabeth Seton had been actively engaged in charitable work among the poor. Now she gathered around her a group of like-minded Catholic women and formed a community, based on the school in Baltimore. By 1812 the community was recognised as an official order under the name of the Daughters of Charity of St Joseph, with Mother Seton as its superior. She became a nun in 1813. By the time she died at Emmitsburg in 1821 more than twenty sister communities had been founded and were running orphanages, hospitals and schools. She was canonized in 1975.

# Bernadette (16 April)

Marie Bernarde Soubirous was born in 1844 in the town of Lourdes, the daughter of a poor miller. She was a delicate child, afflicted with asthma and other ailments, uneducated, and regarded as intellectually rather slow. She was known among her family as Bernadette.

At the age of fourteen, from 11 February 1858 onwards, she had a series of eighteen visions at a shallow cave by the river Gave, near Lourdes. She claimed to see a beautiful young woman who at length announced herself as 'the Immaculate Conception' and who made various communications to her and showed her a forgotten spring of water. Crowds amounting at times to 200,000 began to follow her, but there was no mass hysteria, and although none saw or heard the woman of Bernadette's vision they were impressed by the apparently miraculous appearance of the spring. The last vision was on 16 July and was followed by a fever of religiosity in the district.

Bernadette seems to have hated the attention her experiences drew to her. In 1866 she entered the convent of Notre-Dame de Nevers and played no part in the subsequent development of Lourdes as one of the world's greatest centres of pilgrimage. Continually ailing, she died in 1879 at the age of thirty-five. The Church approached the story of Bernadette with great caution, and when she was canonized in 1933 it was not for her visions, but for her simple piety and trusting faith.

# Frances Cabrini

(13 November)

The first American citizen to be canonized was born at Sant' Angelo Lodigiano in northern Italy in 1850, the youngest of thirteen children. She qualified to be a teacher, but after losing both her parents at the age of twenty felt called to be a nun. She was rejected by two convents on the grounds of ill health, but instead was put in charge of a small orphanage. In 1877 she took her first vows and in 1880 her bishop invited her to start the order of Missionary Sisters of the Sacred Heart, which soon spread across Italy.

Frances herself had wished to be a missionary in China, but Pope Leo XIII urged her to turn her attention instead to the needs of Italian immigrants in the United States. She arrived in New York in 1889 with six of her sisters and spent the next twenty-eight years travelling around North and South America, founding orphanages, schools and convents, and four great hospitals. On visits to Europe she helped to spread the order to eight countries, while in America her work came to extend far beyond the Italian community, even including the convicts of Sing-Sing prison. She became naturalized as an American citizen.

She died in 1917 and was canonized in 1946. In 1950 Pope Pius XII named her the patroness of all immigrants.

# Maximilian Kolbe

(14 August)

Maximilian Kolbe was born in the Polish town of Zdunska-Wola on 17 January 1894. At the early age of thirteen he joined the Conventual Franciscans, and after further study in Poland he was ordained in Rome in April 1918. By then he had already formed the idea of a 'Militia of Mary Immaculate', which he propagated through a journal, *The Knight of the Immaculate*. Another of his visionary ideas was of whole towns populated entirely by friars. One of these, housing 800, was actually set up in Poland and another in Japan, where he had worked for a time, before the Second World War.

In 1940, after the German invasion of Poland, he was arrested, then released. In 1941 he was re-arrested and sent to Auschwitz, where he was treated with great brutality, once being whipped with fifty lashes and left for dead. Surviving these torments, he continued to do what he could for his fellow prisoners. After a successful escape from Block 14, where he was held, the German guards selected ten prisoners for killing as a reprisal, one of them a Polish sergeant who was a family man. Maximilian, then aged forty-seven, offered himself in the sergeant's place. He was the last of the ten to die, having done his best to comfort the other nine. He was canonized in 1982.

# A Calendar of Saints

## January

1  Almachius Concordius, Odilo, Peter of Atroa
2  Basil the Great, Caspar del Bufalo, Macarius the Younger
3  Fulgentius, Geneviève, Joseph Maria Tomasi
4  Elizabeth Bayley Seton
5  John Nepomucene Neumann, Simeon Stylites
6  John de Ribera
7  Lucian of Antioch, Raymund of Penafort
8  Lucian of Beauvais, Severinus of Noricum, Thorfinn
9  Adrian of Canterbury, Philip of Moscow
10  Peter Orseolo
11  Paulinus of Aquileia, Theodosius the Cenobiarch
12  Benedict Biscop, Tatianus
13  Hilary of Poitiers
14  Felix of Nola, Kentigern, Sava (Sabas)
15  Ita, Macarius the Elder, Paul the Hermit
16  Honoratus of Arles
17  Antony the Abbot
18  Deicolus
19  Canute IV, Henry of Uppsala, Wulfstan
20  Euthymius the Great, Eustochio Calafato, Sebastian,
21  Agnes, Meinrad
22  Vincent of Saragossa, Vincent Pallotti
23  John the Almsgiver
24  Francis de Sales, Timothy
25  The Conversion of St Paul
26  Alberic, Eystein, Margaret of Hungary, Paula
27  Angela Merici
28  Thomas Aquinas, Peter Nolasco, Valerius of Saragossa
29  Gildas the Wise, Sulpicius
30  Bathilde, Martina
31  Cyrus and John, John Bosco, Marcella

## February

1  Brigid, Henry Morse
2  Joan de Lestonnac
3  Blaise, Lawrence of Canterbury
4  Andrew Corsini, John de Britto
5  Adelaide of Bellich, Agatha
6  Paul Miki and Companions (Martyrs of Japan)
7  Luke the Younger
8  Jerome Emiliani, John of Matha
9  Appollonia, Cyril of Alexandria, Tèilo
10  Scholastica
11  Benedict of Aniane
12  Julian the Hospitaller, Meletius
13  Katherine dei Ricci
14  Cyril and Methodius, Valentine
15  Sigfrid of Vaxjo
16  Gilbert of Sempringham
17  Finan, The Seven Holy Founders of the Servite Order
18  Colman of Lindisfarne, Theotonius
19  Boniface of Lausanne
20  Wulfric
21  Peter Damian
22  Margaret of Cortona
23  Polycarp
24  Matthias, Praetextatus
25  Ethelbert of Kent, Tarasius, Walburga
26  Alexander of Alexandria
27  Anne Line
28  Oswald of Worcester, Romanus

## March

1  David (Dewi)
2  Agnes of Bohemia, Chad
3  Aelred, Cunegund
4  Casimir of Poland
5  Gerasimus, John Joseph-of-the-Cross
6  Colette, Perpetua and Felicity
7  Drausius, Paul the Simple
8  Felix of Dunwich, John of God, Julian of Toledo
9  Frances of Rome, Gregory of Nyssa, Katherine of Bologna
10  John Ogilvie
11  Eulogius of Cordova, Oengus, Sophronius
12  Theophanes the Chronicler
13  Euphrasia, Gerald
14  Leobinus, Matilda
15  Longinus, Louise de Marillac
16  Abraham Kidunaia, Herbert of Cologne
17  Gertrude of Nivelles, Joseph of Arimathea, Patrick
18  Cyril of Jerusalem, Edward the Martyr
19  Joseph
20  Cuthbert, Martin of Braga, Wulfram
21  Enda, Nicholas von Flüe
22  Nicholas, Owen
23  Benedict the Martyr, Turibius
24  Irenaeus of Sirmium, William of Norwich
25  Alfwold, Lucy Filippini
26  Basil the Younger, Braulio, Felix of Trier
27  John of Damascus, John of Egypt
28  Tutilo
29  Berthold, Mark of Arethusa, Rupert of Salzburg
30  Leonard Murialdo, Osburga, Zosimus of Syracuse
31  Guy of Pomposa

## April

1  Hugh of Grenoble, Macarius the Wonderworker
2  Francis of Paola, Mary the Egyptian
3  Pancras of Taormina, Richard of Wyche
4  Isidore of Seville
5  Vincent Ferrer
6  Eutychius of Constantinople, William of Eskilsoë
7  Celsus of Armagh, John Baptist de la Salle
8  Dionysius of Corinth, Julia Billiart
9  Hugh of Rouen, Waldetrudis
10  Fulbert
11  Gemma Galgani, Stanislaus of Cracow
12  Alferius, Zeno of Verona
13  Hermenegild
14  Bénezet, Bernard of Abbeville
15  Hunna
16  Bernadette, Drogo, Magnus of Orkney
17  Donnan, Robert of Chaise-Dieu, Stephen Harding
18  Apollonius the Apologist, Galdinus
19  Alphege of Canterbury, Leo IX
20  Agnes of Montepulciano, Caedwalla
21  Anselm of Canterbury, Beuno
22  Conrad of Parzham, Theodore of Sykion
23  Adalbert of Prague, George
24  Fidelis of Singmarinen, Ivo, Mellitus
25  Mark
26  Stephen of Perm
27  Anthimus of Nicomedia, Zita
28  Peter Mary Chanel
29  Hugh of Cluny, Joseph Cottolengo, Catherine of Siena
30  Pius V, Wolfhard

# A Calendar of Saints

## May

1. Brieuc, Peregrine Laziosi, Richard Pampuri
2. Athanasius
3. Philip and James
4. Godehard, Pelagia of Tarsus, Robert Lawrence
5. Hilary of Arles
6. Petronax
7. John of Beverley
8. Magdalen of Canossa, Plechelm
9. Pachomius
10. Antoninus of Florence
11. Asaph, Francis di Girolamo, Ignatius of Laconi
12. Germanus of Constantinople, Pancras
13. Andrew Fournet, John the Silent
14. Mary Mazzarello, Michael Garicoïts
15. Dympna, Isidore the Farmer
16. Brendan, Simon Stock
17. Paschal Baylon
18. Eric of Sweden, Felix of Cantalice
19. Dunstan, Ivo of Kermartin
20. Bernardino of Siena, Ethelbert of the East Angles
21. Andrew Bobola, Godric
22. Rita of Cascia
23. Aldhelm, Guibert, Ivo of Chartres, John Baptist Rossi
24. David of Scotland, Vincent of Lérins
25. Madeleine Sophie Barat, Bede
26. Philip Neri
27. Augustine of Canterbury
28. Germanus of Paris
29. William of Toulouse and Companions
30. Joan of Arc
31. Mechtildis of Edelstetten

## June

1. Eneco (Iñigo), Pamphilus of Caesarea
2. Elmo (Erasmus)
3. Charles Lwanga, Joseph Mkasa and Companions
4. Francis Caracciolo, Metrophanes
5. Boniface
6. Jarlath of Tuam, Norbert
7. Antony Gianelli, Colman of Dromore, Meriadoc
8. William of York
9. Columba, Ephraem, Pelagia of Antioch
10. Ithamar
11. Barnabas
12. Eskil, Paula Frassinetti
13. Antony of Padua
14. Methodius of Constantinople
15. Germaine of Pibrac, Vitus
16. John Regis, Lutgard
17. Albert Chmielowski, Botolph
18. Elizabeth of Schönau, Gregory Barbarigo
19. Boniface of Querfurt, Juliana Falconieri
20. Adalbert of Magdeburg, Silverius
21. Alban, Aloysius Gonzaga
22. Paulinus of Nola, Thomas More
23. Joseph Cafasso, Thomas Garnet
24. Bartholomew of Farne, John the Baptist
25. Febronia, William of Vercelli
26. Anthelm
27. Cyril of Alexandria, Ladislas of Hungary
28. Irenaeus of Lyons
29. Peter and Paul
30. The First Martyrs of the Church of Rome, Martial of Limoges

## July

1. Oliver Plunket, Simeon Salus
2. Otto of Bamberg
3. Bernardine Realino, Thomas
4. Elizabeth of Portugal, Odo of Canterbury, Ulric of Augsburg
5. Antony Zaccaria, Athanasius the Anthonite
6. Godelive, Mary Goretti
7. Hedda of Winchester, Palladius
8. Procopius of Caesarea, Withburga
9. Nicholas Pieck and Companions, Veronica Giuliani
10. Antony and Theodosius Pechersky
11. Benedict, Olga
12. Jason, John Gualbert, Veronica
13. Aquilina, Cloelia Barbieri, Francis Solano
14. Camillus de Lellis, Ulric of Zell
15. Bonaventure, Swithin, Vladimir
16. Fulrad, Helier
17. Clement of Okhrida and Companions, Kenelm
18. Bruno of Segni
19. Arsenius, Macrina the Younger
20. Vulmar, Wilgefortis
21. Arbogast, Laurence of Brindisi, Praxedes
22. Philip Evans and John Lloyd, Mary Magdalen
23. Bridget, John Cassian
24. Boris and Gleb, Christina the Astonishing
25. Christopher, James the Greater
26. Ann, Bartholomea Capitanio
27. Pantaleon, Theobald of Marly
28. Samson of Dol
29. Martha, Olaf of Norway
30. Peter Chrysologus
31. Ignatius of Loyola, Neot

## August

1. Ethelwold of Winchester, Peter Julian Eymard
2. Eusebius
3. Germanus of Auxerre, Waltheof
4. John Vianney
5. Addai and Mari, Afra
6. Hormisdas
7. Cajetan, Claudia, Sixtus II
8. Cyriacus, Dominic
9. Oswald of Northumbria
10. Lawrence
11. Attracta, Clare of Assisi
12. Porcarius and Companions
13. Maximus the Confessor, Narses the Gracious, Radegund
14. Maximilian Kolbe
15. Arnulf of Soissons, Blessed Virgin Mary
16. Stephen of Hungary
17. Joan Delanoue, Hyacinth of Cracow, Rock
18. Helen
19. John Eudes, Sixtus III
20. Bernard of Clairvaux, Oswin, Philibert
21. Abraham of Smolensk, Pius X, Sidonius Appollinaris
22. Sigfrid of Wearmouth, Symphorian
23. Philip Benizi, Rose of Lima
24. Audoenus (Ouen), Bartholomew
25. Genesius of Arles, Genesius the Comedian, Louis of France
26. Elizabeth Bichier des Ages
27. Caesarius of Arles
28. Augustine of Hippo, Julian of Brioude, Moses the Black
29. John the Baptist (death of), Medericus (Merry)
30. Margaret Ward, Pammachius
31. Aidan of Lindisfarne, Paulinus of Trier, Raymund Nonnatus

# A Calendar of Saints

## September

1 Drithelm, Fiacre, Giles
2 Brocard, William of Roskilde
3 Cuthburga, Gregory the Great
4 Marinus of San Marino, Rose of Viterbo
5 Bertinus, Lawrence Giustiniani
6 Bega (Bee)
7 Clodoald (Cloud)
8 Adrian, Corbinian
9 Kieran of Clonmacnois, Omer, Peter Claver
10 Nicholas of Tolentino, Pulcheria
11 Deinius, Paphnutius
12 Guy of Anderlecht
13 Eulogius of Alexandria, John Chrysostom
14 Notburga
15 Katherine of Genoa
16 Cyprian, Euphemia, Ninian
17 Hildegard, Lambert of Maastricht
18 Joseph of Cupertino, Methodius of Olympus
19 Emily de Rodat, Theodore of Canterbury
20 The Korean Martyrs
21 Matthew
22 Phocas the Gardener, Thomas of Villanova
23 Adamnan of Iona, Cadoc
24 Gerard of Csanad
25 Albert of Jerusalem, Finnbar, Sergius of Radonezh
26 Cosmas and Damian, Teresa Couderc
27 Elzear of Sabran, Vincent de Paul
28 Eustochium, Wenceslas of Bohemia
29 Archangels Michael and Raphael, Rhipsime, Gaiana and Companions
30 Honorius of Canterbury, Jerome

## October

1 Bavo, Remi, Teresa of Lisieux
2 The Guardian Angels, Leger
3 Gerard of Brogne, Thomas Cantelupe
4 Francis of Assisi
5 Flora of Beaulieu
6 Bruno, Nicetas of Constantinople
7 Justina of Padua, Osyth
8 Keyne, Demetrius, Thais
9 Dionysius (Denis) of Paris, Dionysius the Areopagite, Louis Bertrand
10 Francis Borgia, Paulinus of York
11 Bruno of Cologne, Mary Soledad
12 Ethelburga of Barking, Wilfrid
13 Edward the Confessor, Gerald of Aurillac
14 Callistus (Callixtus) I, Justus of Lyons
15 Euthymius the Younger, Teresa of Avila
16 Gall, Lull, Margaret-Mary
17 Ignatius of Antioch, Seraphino
18 Justus of Beauvais, Luke
19 The Martyrs of North America, Peter of Alcántara
20 Andrew the Cabylite, Bertilla Boscardin
21 Hilarion, John of Bridlington
22 Donatus of Fiesole, Philip and Companions
23 Ignatius of Constantinople, John of Capistrano
24 Antony Claret, Felix of Thibiuca
25 Crispin and Crispinian, Gaudentius of Brescia
26 Cedd
27 Frumentius
28 Faro, Simon and Jude
29 Colman of Kilmacduagh, Theuderius (Chef)
30 Alphonsus Rodriguez, Marcellus the Centurion
31 Foillan of Fosses, Wolfgang

## November

1 All Saints, Benignus of Dijon
2 Marcian
3 Hubert, Martin de Porres, Winifred
4 Charles Borromeo
5 Bertilla, Zachary and Elizabeth
6 Illtyd, Leonard of Noblac, Winnoc
7 Engelbert, Willibrord
8 Godfrey, Willehad
9 Benignus (Benen), Theodore Tiro
10 Andrew Avellino, Justus of Canterbury, Leo the Great
11 Mannas of Egypt, Martin of Tours, Theodore the Studite
12 Josaphat, Nilus the Elder
13 Frances Xavier Cabrini, Nicholas I
14 Dubricius, Lawrence O'Toole
15 Albert the Great, Leopold of Austria, Malo
16 Edmund of Abingdon, Eucharius of Lyons, Margaret of Scotland
17 Elizabeth of Hungary, Gregory of Tours, Hilda, Hugh of Lincoln, Philippine Duchesne
18 Mawes, Odo of Cluny, Romanus of Antioch
19 Barlaam, Narses I
20 Bernward, Edmund the Martyr
21 Albert of Louvain, Gelasius I
22 Cecilia
23 Clement I, Columban
24 Andrew Dung Lac and Companions, Chrysogonus, Colman of Cloyne
25 Mercurius of Caesarea, Moses
26 John Berchmans, Peter of Alexandria, Silvester Gozzolini
27 Fergus of Strathern, Francis Antony of Lucera, James 'the Cut-to-pieces', Virgil of Salzburg
28 James of the March, Katherine Labouré
29 Radbod
30 Andrew, Cuthbert Mayne

## December

1 Edmund Campion, Eligius (Eloi)
2 Chromatius
3 Cassian of Tangier, Francis Xavier
4 John Damascene, Osmund
5 Birinus, Sabas
6 Abraham of Kratia, Nicholas
7 Ambrose
8 Romaric
9 Budoc, Peter Fourier
10 Eulalia of Mérida, Gregory III, Leo the Great
11 Damasus I, Daniel the Stylite
12 Edburga of Minster, Finnian of Clonard, Jane Frances de Chantal
13 Judoc, Lucy, Odilia
14 John of the Cross, Spiridion
15 Mary di Rosa, Nino, Paul of Latros
16 Adelaide
17 Begga, Lazarus, Olympias, Sturmi
18 Flannan, Winebald
19 Anastasius I
20 Dominic of Silos
21 Peter Canisius
22 Chaeremon, Ischyrion and Companions
23 John of Kanti, Thorlac
24 Irminia and Adela
25 Anastasia, Eugenia
26 Stephen
27 Fabiola, John the Divine, Theodore and Theophanes
28 Antony of Lérins, The Holy Innocents
29 Marcellus the Righteous, Thomas Becket, Trophimus of Arles
30 Egwin
31 Columba of Sens, Melania the Younger, Silvester I

# Patron Saints

ACCOUNTANTS: Matthew

ACTORS: Genesius

ADVERTISERS: Bernardino of Siena

AIRMEN AND AIR TRAVELLERS:
Joseph of Cupertino

ANAESTHETISTS: René Goupil

ARCHERS: Sebastian

ARCHITECTS: Barbara

ARGENTINA: Our Lady of Lujan

ARMENIA: Bartholomew

ARTISTS: Luke

ASTRONOMERS: Dominic

ATHLETES: Sebastian

AUSTRALIA:
Our Lady Help of Christians

AUTHORS: Francis de Sales


BAKERS: Elizabeth of Hungary

BANKERS: Matthew

BARBERS: Cosmasand Damian

BARREN WOMEN: Antony of Padua

BAVARIA: Kilian

BEGGARS: Giles

BELGIUM: Joseph

BLACKSMITHS: Dunstan

BLIND PEOPLE:
The Archangel Raphael

BOHEMIA (CZECH REPUBLIC):
Wenceslaus

BOOKKEEPERS: Matthew

BOOKSELLERS: John of God

BOY SCOUTS: George

BRAZIL: Peter of Alcantara

BREWERS:
Augustine; Luke; Nicholas of Myra

BRICKLAYERS: Stephen

BRIDES: Nicholas of Myra

BROADCASTERS: Archangel Gabriel

BUILDERS: Vincent Ferrer; Barbara

BUTCHERS:
Adrian; Luke; Antony the Abbot


CAB DRIVERS: Fiacre

CABINETMAKERS: Anne

CANADA: Anne; Joseph

CANCER VICTIMS: Peregrine Laziosi

CARPENTERS: Joseph

CHARITABLE SOCIETIES:
Vincent de Paul

CHILDREN: Nicholas of Myra

CHILE: James the Greater;
Our Lady of Mount Carmel

CHINA: Joseph

COMEDIANS: Vitus

COOKS: Laurence; Martha

CRIPPLES: Giles

CYPRUS: Barnabas


DANCERS: Vitus

THE DEAF: Francis de Sales

DENMARK: Angsgar; Cnut

DENTISTS; Apollonia

DOMESTIC ANIMALS: Antony

DYSENTERY SUFFERERS: Matrona

EARTHQUAKES: Emygdius

ECOLOGISTS: Francis of Assisi

EDITORS: John Bosco

EMIGRANTS: Frances Xavier Cabrini

ENGINEERS: Ferdinand III

ENGLAND: George

EPILEPTICS: Dympna; Vitus

EXPECTANT MOTHERS:
Gerard Majella

EYE PROBLEMS: Lucy


FALSELY ACCUSED:
Raymund Nonnatus

FARMERS: George; Isidore the Farmer

FATHERS OF FAMILIES: Joseph

FINLAND: Henry of Uppsala

FIREMEN: Florian

FIRE PREVENTION:
Katherine of Siena

FISHERMEN: Andrew, Peter

FLORISTS: Thérèse of Lisieux

FRANCE: Denis; Joan of Arc; Martin;
Remigius (Rémy); Thérèse of Lisieux

FUNERAL DIRECTORS:
Joseph of Arimathea


GARDENERS: Adelard; Fiacre; Phocas

GERMANY: Boniface;
Archangel Michael; Peter Canisius

GLASSWORKERS: Luke

GOLDSMITHS: Dunstan; Anastasius

GRAVEDIGGERS: Antony the Abbot

GREECE: Andrew; Nicholas

GROCERS: Archangel Michael

GUNNERS: Barbara


HAIRDRESSERS: Martin de Porres

HATTERS: James the Less

HEADACHE SUFFERERS:
Teresa of Avila

HEART PATIENTS: John of God

HOSPITALS:
Camillus de Lellis; John of God

HOTELKEEPERS:
Amand; Julian the Hospitaller

HUNGARY: Stephen

HUNTERS: Eustachius; Hubert


INDIA: Our Lady of Assumption

INFANTRYMEN: Maurice

INVALIDS: Roch

IRELAND: Patrick; Brigid; Columba

ITALY: Bernardino of Siena;
Katherine of Siena; Francis of Assisi


JAPAN: Francis Xavier; Peter Baptist

JEWELLERS: Eligius (Eloi); Dunstan

JOURNALISTS: Francis de Sales

KNIGHTHOOD: George


LABOURERS: Isidore

LAWYERS: Thomas More; Yves

LEARNING: Ambrose

LEATHERWORKERS:
Crispin and Crispinian

LIBRARIANS: Jerome

# Patron Saints

LIGHTHOUSE KEEPERS: Dunstan; Venerius

LOCKSMITHS: Dunstan

LOST ARTICLES: Antony of Padua

LOVERS: Valentine

MAIDENS: Katherine of Alexandria

MARINERS: Nicholas of Tolentine

MARRIED WOMEN: Monica

MENTALLY ILL: Dympna

MERCHANTS: Francis of Assisi; Nicholas of Myra

MESSENGERS: Archangel Gabriel

METAL WORKERS: Eligius (Eloi)

MEXICO: Our Lady of Guadalupe

MIDWIVES: Raymund Nonnatus

MILLERS: Arnulph

MISSIONS: Francis Xavier; Thérèse of Lisieux

MOTHERS: Monica

MOTORISTS: Christopher

MOUNTAINEERS: Bernard of Menthon

MUSICIANS: Cecilia; Gregory the Great

NETHERLANDS: Plechelm; Willibrord

NEW ZEALAND: Our Lady Help of Christians

NORWAY: Olaf of Norway

NURSES: Agatha; Camillus de Lellis; John of God

ORPHANS: Jerome Emiliani

PAINTERS: Luke

PARATROOPERS: Archangel Michael

PARIS: Geneviève

PAWNBROKERS: Nicholas of Myra

PERU: Joseph

PHYSICIANS: Luke; Cosmas and Damian; Archangel Gabriel

PILGRIMS: James the Greater

PLASTERERS: Bartholomew

POETS: David; Cecilia

POLAND: Casimir; Cunegund; Hyacinth; Stanislaus; Stephen

POLICEMEN: Archangel Michael

PORTERS: Christopher

PORTUGAL: Francis Borgia; George; Vincent

POSTAL WORKERS: Archangel Gabriel

PREACHERS: Katherine of Alexandria; John Chrysostom

PREGNANT WOMEN: Gerard Majella

PRIESTS: John Vianney

PRINTERS: Augustine; Genesius; John of God

PRISONERS: Dismas

PRISONERS-OF-WAR: Leonard

PUBLIC RELATIONS: Bernardine of Siena

RADIOLOGISTS: Archangel Michael

RHEUMATISM SUFFERERS: James the Greater

ROME: Philip Neri

RUSSIA: Andrew; Boris; Nicholas; Thérèse of Lisieux; Vladimir of Kiev

SAILORS: Brendan; Erasmus (Elmo); Christopher; Cuthbert; Nicholas

SCHOLARS: Brigid

SCIENTISTS: Albert the Great

SCOTLAND: Andrew; Columbus; Margaret

SECRETARIES: Genesius

SHEPHERDS: Drogo

SHOEMAKERS: Crispin and Crispinian

SILVERSMITHS: Andronicus; Dunstan

SINGERS: Cecilia; Gregory the Great

SKATERS: Lidwina

SKIERS: Bernard of Menton

SMITHS: Eligius (Eloi)

SOCIAL WORKERS: Louise de Marillac

SOLDIERS: George; Ignatius of Loyola; Joan of Arc; Martin of Tours; Sebastian

SOUTH AFRICA: Our Lady of Assumption

SPAIN: James the Greater; John of Avila; Teresa of Avila

STONEMASONS: Barbara; Reinhold; Stephen

STUDENTS: Katherine of Alexandria; Thomas Aquinas

SURGEONS: Luke; Cosmas and Damian

SWEDEN: Ansgar; Bridget; Gall; Sigfrid

SWITZERLAND: Gall

TAILORS: Homobonus

TANNERS: Simon; Crispin and Crispinian

TAX COLLECTORS: Matthew

TEACHERS: Gregory the Great; John Baptist de la Salle

TELEPHONE WORKERS: Archangel Gabriel

TELEVISION: Clare of Assisi

TELEVISION WORKERS: Archangel Gabriel

THROAT AFFLICTIONS, SUFFERERS FROM: Blaise

TRAVELLERS: Antony of Padua; Christopher; Julian the Hospitaller; Nicholas of Myra

UNITED STATES: Immaculate Conception

UNIVERSITIES AND SCHOOLS: Thomas Aquinas

VENICE: Mark

WALES: David

WEAVERS: Anastasia; Anastasius; Paul the Hermit

WEST INDIES: Gertrude

WESTMINSTER: Edward the Confessor

WIDOWS: Paula

WINE GROWERS: Morand; Vincent

WINE MERCHANTS: Amand

WOMEN IN LABOUR: Anne

WORKING MEN: Joseph

WRITERS: Francis de Sales; Lucy

YACHTSMEN: Adjutor

L – Z

## CREDITS

8 Martyrdom of St Erasmus, Dieric Bouts (1410/20-1475), Löwen, St Peter AKG

12 John the Baptist, Alexander Andrejevich Ivanov, AKG

14 The Apostle Andrew, Georges de la Tour (1593-1652), Private Collection, AKG

15 St James the Greater, Benvenuto Tisi da Garofalo (1481-1559), Florence, Palazzo Pitti, Bridgeman

16 St Matthew, from the Lindisfarne Gospels (698-700) British Library

17 St Mary Magdalen with St Dominic and St Bernard Nicolas Borras (1530-1610), Bridgeman

18 The Apostle Philip, Georges de la Tour (1593-1652), Norfolk USA, Chrysler Museum, AKG

19 St Peter by William Holman Hunt (1827-1910), Private Collection, Bridgeman

20 The Incredulity of St Thomas, Giovanni Francesco Toscani (1370-1430), Florence, Galleria dell' Accademia, Bridgeman

21 St Mark the Evangelist, Lorenzo Ghiberti (1378-1455), Florence, Baptistery, Bridgeman

22 St Luke, Peter Meghen (1466-1537), Oxford, Corpus Christi College, Bridgeman

23 The Four Apostles by Albrecht Dürer (1471-1528), Munich, Alte Pinakothek, AKG

25 The Miracle of St Barnabas, by Veronese (1528-88), France, Rouen, Musée des Beaux-Arts, Bridgeman

26 Stoning of St Stephen by Gentile da Fabriano (c.1370-1427), Vienna, Kunsthistorisches Museum, Bridgeman

29 The Apostle Paul, Rembrandt (1606-69), Vienna, Kunsthistorisches Museum, AKG

31 St Cecilia, John Melhuish Strudwick (1849-1937), London, Bennie Gray, London, Bridgeman

32 The Martyrdom of St Lawrence, by Agnolo Bronzino (1503-72), Florence, San Lorenzo, Bridgeman

33 St Lawrence, (5th century), Mausoleum Galla Placidia, Ravenna, The Art Archive/Dagli Orti

34 St Anthony Abbot, French School, (15th century), UK, York City Art Gallery, Bridgeman

36 St Helen, British, 15th century, UK, Morley, Church of St Matthew, Bridgeman

38 St George, Giovanni Bellini (c.1430-1516), Italy, Pesaro, Museo Civico, Bridgeman

39 Martyrdom of St Sebastian, Antonio Pollaiuolo (1432/3-98), London, National Gallery, Bridgeman

40-41 St Nicholas rebuking the Tempest, Bicci di Lorenzo (1375-1452), Oxford, Ashmolean Museum, Bridgeman

43, 44 Martyrdom of St Erasmus, Dieric Bouts (1410/20-1475), Löwen, St Peter AKG

45 St Ambrose, Simone Martini (1280-1344) Assisi, S. Francesco, AKG

46 St Basil, Chrysostom and Gregory, (18th century), Minsk, Staatliches Kunstmuseum, AKG

48 St Jerome in his Study, Domenico Ghirlandaio (1449-94), Florence, Ognissanti, Bridgeman

49 Saints Gregory, St Chrysostom and Basil the Great, Byzantine, Art Archive

50 St Augustine, El Greco (1541-1614), Toledo, Art Archive

51 St Augustine, Fra Filippo Lippi (1406-69) Florence, Uffizi, Bridgeman

53 Miracle of St Patrick, Giovanni Battista Tiepolo (1696-1770), Padua, Musei Civici, AKG

54 St Simeon, Russian School (16th century), Moscow, Tretyakov Gallery, Bridgeman

56 St Brigid and Tecla, Llisbjerg, Denmark (12th century), Dagli Orti/Art Archive

57 St Benedict against a Landscape, Signorelli (c.1441-1523), Tuscany, Monte Oliveto Maggiore, Bridgeman

58-59 St Brendan and his crew on a whale, British Library

61 St Brendan, Edward Reginald Frampton (1872-1923), London, Whitman & Hughes, Bridgeman

62 St Columba in Oak Grove, Ireland, Jarrold Publishing/Art Archive

64 Pope Gregory the Great by Carlo Saraceni, (c.1580-1620), Rome, Palazzo Barberini, Bridgeman

68-69 St Augustine, Fra Filippo Lippi (1406-69) Florence, Uffizi, Bridgeman

73 St Cuthbert after his election cures an earl's servant, British Library

74 St Boniface, Alfred Rethel (1816-59), Berlin, Nationalgalerie, Bridgeman

77 Saints Cyril and Methodius, mosaic, Rome, San Clemente Basilica, Dagli Orti/Art Archive

80 St Wenceslas, Czech School (16th century), Czech Rep., Nelahozeves Castle, Bridgeman

81 St Dunstan Writing, British Library

83 King Stephen, Pierre Joseph Verhaghen (1728-1811), Crimea, Natural History Museum, Dagli Orti/Art Archive

85 Edward the Confessor, Jean de Boulogne Giambologna (1529-1608), Florence, San Marco, Bridgeman

86 St Bruno, Pier Francesco Mola (1612-66), Alywick Castle, Northumberland, Bridgeman

89 St Bernard, Abbot of Clairvaux, Jean Fouquet (c.1420-80), France, Chantilly, Musée Conde, Giraudon/Bridgeman

90 The Vision of St Hildegard, Battista Dossi (c.1474-1548), Florence, Uffizi, Bridgeman

92 Murder of Thomas Becket, from a book of Psalms (13th century), British Library, Bridgeman

93 St Thomas Becket, Girolamo da Santacroce (1556-?), Venice, S. Silvestro, AKG

94 Bust of St Dominic, Catalan School (c.1450), Christie's Images, Bridgeman

96 St Francis of Assisi preaching to the birds (panel), Giotto di Bondone (c.1266-1337), Louvre, Bridgeman

99 St Louis of France, Flemish School (15th century), Louvre, AKG

101 St Thomas Aquinas, Sandro Botticelli (1444/5-1510), Switzerland, Riggisberg, Abegg Collection, Bridgeman

102-103 St Catherine of Siena, Gerolamo di Benvenuto (1470-1542), USA, Fogg Museum, Bridgeman

105 The Mystic Marriage of St Catherine of Siena, Fra Bartolomeo (1475-1517), Louvre, AKG

107 Joan of Arc, Dante Gabriel Rossetti (1828-82), London, Christie's Images, Bridgeman

108 Sir Thomas More, Hans Holbein the Younger (1497/8-1543), London, Philip Mould, Historical Portraits Ltd, Bridgeman

110 St Ignatius of Loyola, French School (17th century), Chateau de Versailles, Bridgeman

112 St Francis Xavier, Nicolas Poussin (1594-1665), Louvre, Dagli Orti/Art Archive

113 St Teresa of Avila, Juan de la Miseria (c.1526-1616), Avila, Spain, Convent of St Teresa, Bridgeman

114 St Philip Neri, Guiseppe Angeli (1712-98), Venive, Ca Rezzonico, Dagli Orti/Art Archive

116 St John of the Cross, Spanish School (18th century), Private Collection, Bridgeman

117 St Francis of Sales, Bishop of Geneva, Giambattista Tiepolo (1696-1770), Udine, Museo Civico, Dagli Orti/Art Archive

118 St Vincent de Paul and the Sisters of Charity, Jean Andre (1662-1753), Hopitaux de Paris, Bridgeman

## INDEX of major entries